The making of writers is mysterious. Much of our schooling takes place out of school, as you'll see in this account of my writerly beginnings. Though you won't find tragedy or trauma here, my path to publication was anything but straight. The pastimes I pursued and the detours I took might look like colossal wastes of time. But. . . .

"A well-written and engaging work that will inspire young readers and writers."
—*School Library Journal*

"An inspiring look at how an award-winning author eventually found his voice."
—*Publishers Weekly*

NO MAP, Great Trip

A YOUNG WRITER'S ROAD TO PAGE ONE

PAUL FLEISCHMAN

Greenwillow Books
An Imprint of HarperCollins*Publishers*

The text of this book is set in 12-point Century Schoolbook.
Book design by Paul Zakris

Library of Congress Cataloging-in-Publication Data

Names: Fleischman, Paul, author.
Title: No map, great trip : a young writer's road to page one /
by Paul Fleischman.
Description: First edition. | New York, NY : Greenwillow Books, an
imprint of HarperCollins Publishers, [2019] | Audience: Ages 8-12. |
Audience: Grades 4-6.
Identifiers: LCCN 2018052592 | ISBN 9780062857460 (paperback)
Subjects: LCSH: Fleischman, Paul—Juvenile literature. |
Authors, American—Biography—Juvenile literature.
Classification: LCC PS3556.L42268 Z46 2019 | DDC 811/.54 [B] —dc23
LC record available at https://lccn.loc.gov/2018052592

20 21 22 23 24 PC/LSCH 10 9 8 7 6 5 4 3 2 1
First Greenwillow paperback edition, 2020

 Greenwillow Books

For my father and mother

Contents

Listening in on the world from my bedroom

1

Voices in the Night

I'm ten years old and have the glittering good luck
to live across the alley from a man who works for
a toy company. He needs a boy to pose for a photo
in the company's catalog. In exchange, the boy can
pick any one item from its pages. Am I interested in
being such a boy?

Am I ever. The photo shoot takes minutes, but
I spend an eternity with the thick catalog. It's like
a mile-long candy counter. I dawdle for days, then

finally decide on the shortwave radio.

In truth, it's a kit, a collection of parts that could conceivably become a shortwave radio. The neighbor brings it over after work, but assembling it is beyond me. If my parents are less than thrilled with inheriting this task, they don't show it. Maybe they're attracted by the challenge. They've recently taught themselves to lay bricks and graft trees. They clear off a table and dig in.

They'll need a lot of tools, including a soldering iron and flux to join wire to metal. Fortunately, it's 1962, an era when calling a plumber or electrician is a last resort. My aunt Dorothy has a drill press, band saw, and anvil. Of course my parents own a soldering iron.

They spend days decoding the instructions. They wind copper wire around coils, screw part X to Y, then solder CC to DD, a puff of smoke rising from the soldering iron's work site.

At last the radio is finished. I'm buzzing with high-voltage excitement. It has five different bands. For an antenna, my father runs a length of copper wire from the peak of the roof into my bedroom window and affixes it to the back of the set. My mother and two sisters gather around. I turn it on.

Suddenly, voices that had been whizzing imperceptibly around us are audible. We hear transmissions from a dispatcher to police cars. Then offshore fishermen talking to their wives on land.

"Yeah."

Long pause.

"Pretty good."

Longer pause.

"Maybe Wednesday."

For some reason, we can only hear the fishermen's side of the conversation. They don't talk much.

We try a different band and are plunged into a strange land of electronic beeps and burbles. We find a station that sounds like a ticking clock. Every five minutes it announces the time. Strange. We creep cautiously ahead, hear Morse code, pass through another forest of static, then make out a male voice speaking English.

"That concludes the news from Radio Havana Cuba."

We've got Cuba! The shortwave really can pick up stations from other countries.

Cuba is only ninety miles from the U.S. Can we hear something farther away? We try another band. On the hour we hear the slow tolling of a bell. Then a female voice announces, "You're listening to the foreign service of the BBC."

The British Broadcasting Corporation! My parents say that the bell is the famous Big Ben in London. *We're hearing England!*

I'm wowed. My world until now has been Santa Monica, California: school, the beach, Los Angeles beyond. But the shortwave allows spirit travel. Later that night I'm listening to Australia. Then to a Canadian Broadcasting Corporation announcer, who's reading letters sent by listeners to be shared over the air to family living beyond mail delivery in the country's far north.

In the morning, I see written down on the legal pad by the radio the frequencies my father frequented after I went to sleep:

10:00	11450	Radio Berlin International
10:20	11825	New Zealand?
10:45	15165	The Voice of the Andes—Quito, Ecuador

I put a world map up on my wood-paneled wall and stick flag pins in the capitals of countries I've heard.

More important, I get a copy of the *World Radio Handbook*. This holds something crucial about stations: their addresses. Shortwave listeners send reception reports to stations, giving the date, time, frequency, the program heard, and how strong the signal was. This is useful to stations. In return, they send postcard-sized confirmations to listeners, called QSL cards. Shortwave buffs cherish their collections, especially cards from hard-to-hear stations.

I already collect coins and stamps, but QSL cards come with an added lure: getting stuff in the mail. I begin mailing out reception reports. Long weeks pass. Then the first QSL arrives. It's in an envelope that also has a station decal. Cool!

More drift in, accompanied by maps, brochures, station schedules, flags. I've barely gotten a letter in my life, but now I'm getting nearly as much mail as my parents. Radio Peking sends me a medallion engraved with the head of China's ruler, Mao Zedong. We get Christmas cards that year from radio stations in Indonesia, East Germany, Argentina.

A QSL card from Australia

On TV, everyone is white and either riding a horse or living happily in the suburbs. There are only three national television networks, all similar. But the shortwave opens windows onto hundreds of different cultures.

I listen to programs devoted to Caribbean music, the cricket scene in India, saunas in Finland. I like to stay up late at night and listen to Arabic music, which arrives in waves from the other side of the globe. No such music can be heard on KRLA or the other stations Los Angeles listens to.

Shortwave stations broadcast in many languages, but I only speak English. What are you hearing if you don't know the meaning of the words? Their music. French flows like water. Russian sounds like a train wreck of consonants. I often have no idea what language I'm hearing but keep listening for a while just for the pleasure of the sound.

I like Santa Monica. I enjoy school. I'm funny, popular, and the next year will be elected the president of my grammar school. But the shortwave reveals a need for novelty and variety that I didn't know I had. I like leaping over Santa Monica's borders and listening in on life in places I've never seen. In a few years, I'll want to do more than just listen.

Most countries have a government-sponsored shortwave station. The United States's station is called the Voice of America. I notice that the news heard there sounds just like the news on AM radio and TV. But Radio Peking calls our armed forces fighting in Vietnam "paper tigers" and paints us as losing. Until then, I'd only heard positive news about our involvement in Vietnam. This jolts me.

The newscasters in Havana praise Cuba's leader,

Fidel Castro, who's allied with our enemies, the Russians. I've heard only bad things about both, but the announcers describe advances in agriculture and steeply rising literacy rates. Can this be true?

The civil rights movement is in full swing, not only in the U.S. but in South Africa. There, Nelson Mandela has been sentenced to life imprisonment for fighting against segregation. On Radio South Africa, I hear programs describing how happy Blacks are with their separate lives. The announcer's voice sounds caring and sincere. I'm older now and suspect he's lying. Kids lie as required, but adults are supposed to keep strictly to the truth. It's disturbing to witness.

The red-flagged pins multiply on the world map. We buy a more powerful shortwave with an alluring array of needled dials and tuning knobs. After discovering that stations in Asia come in better in the early morning, I begin tuning in to the Far East before school. At night, I like to sit in the dark and listen through headphones, the lit dials the only light in the room.

One night in 1967 I'm combing the bands for new stations when I hear a faint male voice in strongly accented English. The man seems panicked. He describes a military attack, apparently on his station. His voice continually fades out, then returns. Stations usually identify themselves every half hour. The top of the hour arrives, but there's no announcement. I wait thirty more minutes. Still no ID. And then it comes: Radio Biafra, in Africa.

The man is broadcasting from the part of Nigeria that's trying to secede. The Biafran War and the starvation that results will cause millions of deaths. The fear in his voice is unmistakable, a universal emotion that makes for instant connection despite the distance and the difference in our circumstances. I have trouble sleeping that night. In the morning I wonder if the man is still alive. I return to the frequency where I found him but never hear the station again.

The making of writers is mysterious. Much of our schooling takes place out of school, as you'll see in this account of my writerly beginnings. Though you won't find tragedy or trauma here, my path to publication was anything but straight. The pastimes I pursued and the detours I took might look like colossal wastes of time. But consider the shortwave.

The exposure to other cultures planted the seeds for the multinational cast in *Seedfolks*.

Listening to Hindi and Swedish and Swahili showed me the musical side of language, leading to the poetic duets in *Joyful Noise* and a Newbery Medal.

The descriptions of distant places would help launch me on the trip that would be transformed into *Whirligig*.

The realization that history was happening in front of me inspired *Dateline: Troy* and *Eyes Wide Open* decades later.

Most important of all was the long-term effect of hearing Radio Biafra that night. But I'm getting ahead of myself. My charmed childhood had more than just a shortwave. A year or two after it crackled to life, another newcomer joined the family. One who was old. With only one arm. One who gave me brand-new eyes.

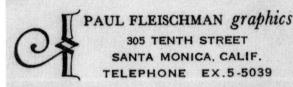

One of my business labels

2

Printer's Devil

My parents drive home one day with the car crammed with cargo of a sort I've never seen. We all help unload. Into the house come wide wooden drawers divided into compartments, a cabinet to hold them, a heavy slab of marble, bags of wooden blocks, boxes filled with bits of lead. Last to emerge is the queen bee of this hive of equipment, a hand printing press.

My father, Sid Fleischman, has been a magician, journalist, Hollywood screenwriter, and author of adventures with titles like *Murder's No Accident* and *Danger in Paradise*. But the novel he wrote as a lark for my sisters and me has led him into a new realm he's discovered he likes: children's books.

His books for young readers are set in the 1800s. Authors need to know their characters' lives in detail, but daily life a century or more in the past was utterly different. How do you find out what people ate for dinner in 1849? Back before the internet, you go to the library.

My father checks out histories, diaries, novels. The books are stacked on the piano, then disappear one by one into his study. There he goes through them looking for the information he needs, copying it into his research notebook. I've looked through it.

The price of a bath in San Francisco during the Gold Rush? An astronomical ten dollars.

Dinner in the gold diggings? Bear steak and sowbelly-and-beans, washed down with coffee, known there as Jamoka.

When Praiseworthy, the proper butler in my father's Gold Rush novel, *By the Great Horn Spoon!*, is challenged by a miner to a fight, he feels honor bound to confess his advantage: he's read *The Gentleman's Book of Boxing*. I grow up knowing that you can learn anything from books, just as my father did.

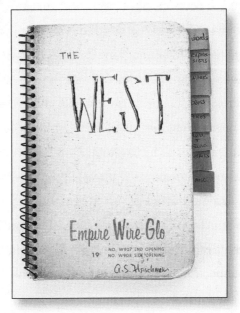

One of my father's research notebooks, with tabs for words, dress, prices, flora and fauna, and more

My sisters and I are his assistants. When he finishes a chapter, he reads it aloud to us all. He notices where we laugh or don't, makes notes in the margin, asks if something was clear or confusing.

During the writing of *Mr. Mysterious & Company*, his first children's book, he once asked us what we thought should happen to the traveling magician and his family who starred in the story. I suggested they get lost. To my amazement, that's exactly what occurred a chapter later. My younger sister—who perhaps wasn't enjoying her piano lessons—had lobbied to have their piano burn down. This suggestion wasn't acted upon. Crowdsourcing can be cruel.

We aren't my father's only helpers. My mother helps supply him with names, something writers need by the barrelful. My father might turn down hundreds before finding one that feels just right. He got Praiseworthy's from a funeral-home billboard. Like a miner working a stream, my mother gathers the gold from articles and obituaries in the *Los Angeles Times*, saving the best in a notebook for my father:

Opal Crunk

Blanche Brockledank

Sir Basil Smallpiece

My aunt Dorothy, three hundred miles north, has the same gene. She works the watershed drained by the *Monterey Herald* and sends my father her annotated finds:

Ricardo Macadangdang (former resident of Salinas)

Fawnda Fauble (survivor in obit)

Skip Raring (opponent of motorcycle helmet law)

She supplies him as well with unusual place names (Enigma, Georgia) and business names (Finger of God Cement Works in Ghana). She's a champion recorder. She writes down rainfall amounts and graphs high and low temperatures at her house. When she and I stop to get gas for her Thunderbird, she enters the number of gallons and the odometer reading in a notebook. Writing can preserve anything. I catch the love of notebooks. I don't have anything to write down, but wish I did.

Books are great teachers, but some things are best learned in person. Before *By the Great Horn Spoon!* was written, we drove to the Sierra foothills and visited museums and historical sites, my father scratching notes like a waiter. We bought gold pans and tried our luck in a stream. No fortunes were made. Maybe that's why Praiseworthy and Jack found a different route to riches: washing gold dust from the hair trimmings under their barbering chair.

A few years later, my father was writing a book about a boy's adventures rounding up his siblings in the wake of the Civil War. The boy will raise chickens on an Ohio River raft, so we raised a pair ourselves.

The chicks, not long after arriving

My sisters and I helped build the coop. When my father photographed the chicks, we held up a yardstick to show the birds' heights as well as a card giving their ages, information he needed for his descriptions. Long after *Chancy and the Grand Rascal* was published, those chickens were still giving us eggs. Research has unexpected rewards.

So it is that we're now unloading an entire print shop from our Ford Galaxie. My father's next book will star a tramp printer, the sort who brought his wagon to a stop in a new town, put out a newspaper where there might never have been one, and moved on when the urge struck, or possibly a bullet from a reader of his editorials.

It was time for more firsthand research. My parents decide to learn how to print. My sisters and I decide we will, too.

Until the late 1800s, printed matter started with individual lead letters plucked from a typecase, lined up in a composing stick, then locked into a press, inked, and touched against paper. The linotype machine and then the computer replaced this method, but hobbyists and makers of fine books kept the skills alive. Deep in the classifieds in the *Los Angeles Times*, my mother found someone selling everything needed. We are the happy buyers.

The press is installed in a workroom in the backyard. My father assembles the type cabinet and puts it in our house's all-purpose room. We label the compartments in the type cases and begin putting each P and Q and comma in its proper place. Immediately, we begin speaking a language no one else on our block speaks.

En quads are the plugs of lead used to separate

words. *Furniture* isn't couches or chairs, but the blocks of wood used to hold type in the iron *chase*. A *key* doesn't unlock a door, but tightens the furniture in the chase.

Setting type—specifically the word typesetting

Along with new words comes a new skill: learning to read backward. A mirror produces a reversed image; so does inked paper. Type has to be arranged right to left so as to come out left to right. Holding the composing stick in my left hand, I pick out the letters and spaces from the typecase and line them up from right to left. After a few weeks, reading backward feels nearly natural.

My sisters and I want our own stationery. To get

it requires making a lot of choices. What font? What size? Name in all capitals, or caps and lowercase? How much space between the name and address? Should there be a line between them? I'm unaware that I'm getting practice answering the sort of open-ended questions—the kind with no right answer—that artists of all types constantly confront.

Not that I feel called to a career in the arts. Though my father is a writer, I don't lie awake imagining my name sideways on the spines of books. I'm not a big reader and won't begin devouring books for pleasure until high school. I'm too busy with peashooter wars with my friends, learning to throw the just-invented Frisbee, skim-boarding at the beach—and messing around with lead type.

When the typesetting is finished, I do a test using carbon paper. If the letters look too close together, I put tiny slivers of brass between them all. If that's too much space, I take them all out and put in thinner slivers of copper. It's time-consuming. Nothing comes out perfectly the first time. I have no idea that slow and careful will be the hallmarks of my writing process.

"Imagine setting an entire newspaper," says my father. "Every week."

The thought is daunting. Printers had help, though. A *printer's devil* was a boy who earned a few pennies helping set all that type. A boy like me.

The most exciting stage is the actual printing. I dip a palette knife into the can of buttery black ink and spread some on the press's circular platen. Pulling down on the press's handle lifts the rubber rollers and coats them with ink. When the type and paper are put into place, those rollers ink the letters, the letters meet the paper—and voilà—the magic of printed words. We're as giddy as Gutenberg.

A printing press much like ours

I'm a big fan of *Batman* on TV. Using a lead ornament of a bat, I print *Batman Rules* on notebook paper, to the mystification of my teachers. My sisters and I print half sheets of paper reading *From the desk of* followed by our names. We press them tightly together in a padding press, spread on a special glue, and end up with pads of stationery. Mission accomplished. But how many letters do kids write? Adults, though, are a different story.

One of my parents' friends hires me to print his stationery. Then envelopes for his work. Then business cards. My fame spreads through an office of Beverly Hills psychiatrists. Suddenly I'm in business.

I print up my own labels to put on finished boxes of cards and envelopes. I call my business Paul Fleischman Graphics and keep a ledger book. By today's standards, prices are shockingly cheap. For five hundred printed envelopes, I charge only $2.50. I'm not getting rich, but my left arm is sure getting strong from pulling the press's handle. I get a lot of practice designing and revising. Later in life these will be translated into outlining and editing.

At night I distribute the type back into its compartments while my parents read up on bookbinding. As a trial, they publish my whimsical essay, "Raising Vultures for Fun and Profit," as a 2-x-3–inch booklet. My mother learns to marble paper, touching it down onto swirls of oily pigments floating on water. The result is an intricate landscape of curves and colors. She uses this for the book's endpapers.

Getting to name your publishing house is one of the joys of owning a press. My parents settle on The Pennyroyal Press and buy an ornament of a flower resembling pennyroyal. They print a collection of children's poems by a friend and several other palm-sized productions.

Like a tramp printer, we can now send our opinions out into the world. When Shirley Temple, a famous former child actress, is named one of the U.S. delegates to the United Nations General Assembly, the news seems too outlandish to be true. Playing off the phrase "surely you jest," we use a font of huge wooden type to print a bumper sticker proclaiming SHIRLEY YOU JEST. Ours is the only car in the universe that wears it.

I might not be a big reader, but I do look at type catalogs. These show scores of fonts of type, each

SHIRLEY YOU JEST

*Never did a bumper sticker
have a smaller print run—three copies*

with its own personality: stately Palatino, haughty Hadriano, funny Hickory, whose letters look as if they're built out of branches. It's an exciting day when we drive downtown to enter the Los Angeles Type Company. We wander the vast, dimly lit space, perhaps buying a new font, maybe a new color of ink, and search through the innumerable ornaments: pointing fingers in scores of different styles, banners, arrows, cats arching, eagles flying. My sisters and I drop the ones we covet into paper bags.

I keep my business going into high school. My father is still grappling with the novel about the printer, a wrestling match that will continue off and on for years. The book is finally published as *Humbug Mountain*, a place name he found in a history of the American West. Neither of us know that the trip I've slowly been working up to will take me to the actual Humbug Mountain.

WRITING KNOW-HOW

Why You Need a Pocket

Why should you bother with research? Because it's details that convince readers that your created world is real. And if they believe it's real, they're more likely to accept your cast and plot as real, too.

That's why "Write what you know" is the advice aspiring writers hear most. The best way to get those myriad details right—from shoe styles to slang to the route of the #12 bus—is to write about the world you know.

Does this mean you're condemned to stick to times and places you've lived in? Not at all.

Writers of fantasy and science fiction construct whole worlds they've never inhabited. Better advice for them would be, "Write what you can convincingly invent," with the emphasis on *convincing*. If the history, geography, society, and other details of your realm feel related and consistent, you have a good chance of getting readers to accept them.

If your story is set in the past, I'd change the advice to "Write what you can find out." Before putting down a word of *Bull Run*, I combed dozens of books about the battle and the Civil War in general, my eye out for telling details: that horses were groomed an hour above the knee and an hour below, that salt pork fried in rancid grease was soldiers' staple food, that berries were ripe along the road on that fateful day in July.

Books set in the present require research as well. I wanted to write about the founding of a community garden in *Seedfolks* but had never been part of one. It also happened that there weren't any nearby. So I both read about them and visited them wherever I was traveling, jotting down details: a garden plot furnished with the back seat of a car, a brick walkway, the barbed wire that made a prominent appearance in the novel. Real life will give you details that no research book will include. Like my father, I also tried firsthand experience, planting a long row of beans and taking notes on their journey from seedlings to side dish.

Writers on a research mission go looking for facts but often come back with fiction: ideas for scenes, new characters, plot twists. When a community gardener told me that some people were illegally selling the produce they raised, I built a fictional character around that fact. Details not only support your work, but can end up expanding and improving your story.

That's why I take notes on all kinds of experiences that come my way, from tours of historic houses to jury duty to the time I helped butcher a pig. To capture those details, I always wear a shirt with a pocket. Inside there's always pen and paper. All hail the humble pocket!

My first pocket notebook

My childhood mitt

3
Disorganized Sports

One day, in the trash can of a man rumored to play minor league baseball, I find a wooden bat. It's as huge and heavy as a caveman's club, with a chunk missing from its massive barrel. I carry it home.

With difficulty. The reason: I'm the smallest boy in my class all the way from first grade to eleventh. If you want to find me in a group photo, simply look at the front row, then check the ends. Adults' faces peer down from high altitude. So do those of

many of my classmates. Depending on hairstyle,
I'm a millimeter taller, the same height as, or
humiliatingly shorter than my younger sister.

My short stature sometimes seems the central
fact about me. At other times, I forget it entirely.
Though I sense that I'll never swing a bat like the
one I've found, there will be games aplenty in my
life, despite zero minutes playing organized sports.
Disorganized sports are a different matter.

I love baseball. The boy who hits the longest
home runs at my elementary school isn't the brawn-
iest, but a skinny kid who simply has impeccable
coordination. There's hope. I put my Keyston mitt
between my mattress and box spring to help it live
up to the *V-Hinge* printed on the leather.

It also bears the words *Professional Model*, but in
fifth grade my friends and I come up with a decidedly
unprofessional spin on the game. We transpose it to
the school's tennis court, with the great advantage
that now only two players are needed. The pitcher
flings a tennis ball toward the batter in the court's
corner. Grounders and balls hit into the net are outs.
Over the net is a single, off the fence is a double,
over the fence is a home run. Errant pitches don't

leave bruises, and the ball carries pleasingly, such that even the puny can hit homers. It's a blast.

In elementary school P.E. is fun, but in junior high it feels like part of military training. We're publicly measured and weighed at the start of each semester. We climb ropes like commandos. The gravel-voiced instructors put us through bizarre calisthenics, demanding we lift our chins to our chests fifty times while lying on our backs. "You want a big bull neck, don't you?" one bellows. Not really, I think.

It's laughable. But teenaged boys think practically anything is funny. I love the way *Mad* magazine mocks everything from movies to politics. Following suit, my friends and I play games that make fun of games and the people who take them so seriously.

We invent Skrugby, which is like football but played with the long fruit of a plant that grows in some of our front yards. It's shaped like a huge ear of corn, difficult to throw with a spiral but better than a football for handing off. We concoct complicated scoring rules, funny names for plays, cryptic signal-calling schemes. We move the game from our front yards to Douglas Park, where we play across the low chain-link fence from the exceedingly dignified lawn bowling club. Its gentlemen and ladies, dressed in white pants and skirts, stare at our antics in bafflement.

When we get tired of this, we make up a game that's essentially soccer played with a chalk eraser in front of the tennis backboards. We call this Skrugby, too. Jocks look on but don't lower themselves to compete. Perfect.

We then devise a form of basketball that favors the short and quick over the tall. We steal, we pass constantly, but we rarely shoot. We go up for a layup but pass at the last moment. We're like gnats in constant motion, keeping the ball away from the giants on the other team. It drives our P.E. coaches mad.

We're not the only ones relying on speed instead of strength. The Dodgers are doing the same in baseball. Their speedy leadoff hitter, Maury Wills, might bunt his way to first base, steal second and third, and come home on a groundout, without a ball ever leaving the infield. Sandy Koufax tosses another shutout, and the Dodgers win 1-0. They ride this style to the World Series the year I'm eleven, beating the Yankee sluggers four games to none.

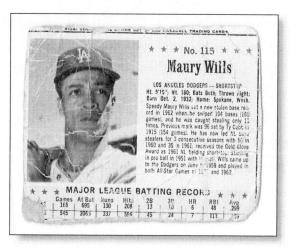

My hero

Games are more than just games. Might makes right in many spheres, but most of us want good, not ruthlessness, to triumph. That's why we root for David instead of Goliath, for Harry Potter and Katniss and the New York Mets—who'd known only losing seasons until they found themselves in the 1969 World Series. "Kids have a strong sense of justice," my father says one day, and the remark sticks with me.

To take a break from writing, he usually works in the yard, but sometimes he watches roller derby on TV. *Roller derby?* It sounds strange, but makes perfect sense to me now. There were the good guys—the Los Angeles Thunderbirds, with their pint-sized star, Ralphie Valladares. Opposite were the evil opponents, known to trip, cheat, and get away with it. The opponents always shot out to a huge lead, celebrating their dirty play with grins. But the Thunderbirds nearly always bounced back, with Valladares usually leading them to a last-second victory.

This was more fiction than sport, and my father studied it as if reading another author's work. His conclusions: a nasty villain is a good thing, right needs to beat might, but the victory can't be easy.

My mother fights for underdogs in the real world. She and a friend operate a nonprofit that gives away books to students in underserved schools. She volunteers in a Veterans Administration garden, showing PTSD sufferers how to grow vegetables and flowers—a major inspiration for *Seedfolks*. Fluent in Spanish, she tutors newcomers in English. I follow her lead decades later, volunteering in a middle-school ELL class where I meet the model for the *Seedfolks* character Gonzalo.

My mother is a crack ping-pong player who enjoys my variation of the game in which the ball can be hit off the wall that runs beside the table. Hatching and altering games is great training for hatching entire worlds. The games Wesley concocts in *Weslandia* are the direct descendants of Skrugby, but so is his entire civilization. In the realms we invent, justice can triumph and brains can beat brawn—inspiring some to work for change in the real world around them. Make-believe is more than child's play.

Taking my turn at the helm

4
Water World

Every family is its own world. Mine loves animals, testified by our dog, cat, two chickens, two rabbits, tortoise, and a jay my mother has tamed.

We're also word people. There are long discussions about whether the proper usage is "get a haircut," "have a haircut," or "take a haircut." When *Saturday Review* arrives in the mail every week, my mother turns to the cryptogram at the back of the magazine and copies it on a sheet of paper so that she and my father can race in solving it. Behind them, we watch *"KZPM BT YZPU GXA VLFA GXA."*— *ZTEFP KBJRU* reveal itself to be *"Work is more fun than fun."*—Oscar Wilde.

Magic is a prominent motif in our house, from the posters of famous magicians on the walls to my father's magic friends who come to dinner. The highlight of every birthday party is the human skull that my father brings out. Using his ventriloquist skills, he invites kids to ask questions, which the skull, its movable jaw clacking, answers.

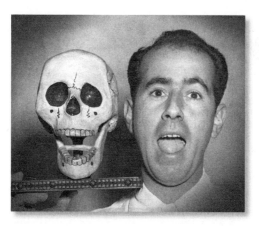

My father and his assistant

We're also gardeners. My parents dig up more and more of the lawn to make way for fruit trees, berries, vegetables, and then an entire cornfield in the front yard, the only one on view in Santa Monica. Each night at dinner, my parents count up the number of items on the table that they've grown. No wonder my father writes a whole series about Josh McBroom's wonderful one-acre farm, and that I become the author of *Weslandia*. When my mother finds a tomato worm on one of our vines, she puts it on her palm and whistles for the jay. It's a win-win-lose.

We not only have a shortwave and a printing press, but a telescope and a microscope. But there's something missing that other families do and we don't. They travel.

My parents have already done that. My father toured the country with a magic troupe during the Depression, and he and my mother have both lived in Mexico City and Manhattan. World War II took my father to China and back. Later my parents traveled through Europe and would have settled there were it not for a problem—me. My mother was pregnant and had complications that cut the trip short.

Apparently, they've seen all they need to. My father has walked the sands of Tahiti, Mazatlán, and the French Riviera, and declares Santa Monica's beaches to be the world's prettiest. Why go anywhere else?

Because my friends tell tales of driving to Yosemite and Yellowstone, of canoeing on the Great Lakes, of seeing bears and bald eagles. True, we once visited Sequoia National Park and the Grand Canyon. But otherwise it's as if the earth ends at Santa Monica's borders. My sisters and I not only never gape at the Rockies, we never set eyes on the Hollywood Bowl.

But then my parents tell us they're considering a trip, one they think we'll like. They show us a brochure. It's from Havalark, a company that rents houseboats. We're going to live on the water for a week in the California Delta, where the Sacramento and San Joaquin Rivers merge before entering San Francisco Bay. It's a trip that will open my borders in thrilling fashion.

Lists are made. Huge maps are ordered, with the land in yellow and the rivers in blue, the water sprinkled with depth readings. Best of all, the family across the street, with three kids our ages, will rent a houseboat at the same time.

It's a full day's drive north to Stockton, the hot hours worth it when we see our boat. It's got a full-length flat roof you can put chairs on. Inside, it's like a cleverly made toy, with storage compartments high and low and hidden beds popping into view. Not an inch is wasted. The tiny bathroom is actually a shower: just close the toilet lid and turn on the water.

We won't simply live on the water—we'll move. We've got engines, anchors, and a radio. My father loved cruising through the South Pacific in the navy. He fires up the twin engines, and our group's two boats head down the sparkling San Joaquin.

I'm thirteen and have grown up near the beach but have almost never set foot on a boat. This one boasts no sailboat's graceful curves. It's a rectangle straight out of a geometry textbook, but who cares? Powering up the widening channel, rounding mysterious bends, then tying up to a stout tree for the night, listening to the river sounds coming in the window before falling asleep on the dining area's vinyl cushions . . . it's kid heaven.

I've come with rod, reel, and a heavy tackle box. There are striped bass and sturgeon here, and giant catfish lurking on the bottom. I'm determined to bring them aboard and spend hours fishing from the roof or in its shade below. I cast, wait, reel in, adjust sinkers and bait, and cast again. And again. And again. The Havalark brochure shows a boy landing something huge. My experience is otherwise.

This catfish toddler was probably as surprised to be caught as I was to catch him.

Fortunately, we've brought plenty of food. When grub and gas run low, there are markets and gas stations right on the water to serve boat traffic. Though we kids take turns at the wheel in open water, dealing with the powerful currents makes docking a challenge. At those times my father calls out our position, and my mother expertly guides the boat to the dock, my father stepping ashore and tying our lines to the cleats. It's different than driving to the store.

And even more different when we come to a bridge. When that happens, we give our horn a blast. The head of the bridge keeper peers our way from his window. Barriers come down, stopping car traffic. Then, with a great clanking racket, the middle of the bridge rises so we can pass under. We thank him with a pair of toots on our horn.

One of the movable bridges we encountered

The delta is a maze of channels. We pick our way through them, steaming up the Sacramento

to Locke, once a hub for Chinese laborers but now nearly a ghost town. We pass places whose names go on my father's list: Old River, False River, Little Potato Slough. In the late afternoons we tie up, boat to boat, the adults gathering on one and the kids on the other. When my father's film agent and his family join us on a third boat, we have a true convoy.

The trip lasts a week. But we have so much fun that we do it again over Christmas eighteen months later. This time it's cold by California standards and we have the water to ourselves. We've brought a tabletop Christmas tree in a pot and open presents at the dining-room table. Our boat on this trip has a second-deck wheelhouse that lets you look far over the flat country. I've read Mark Twain's *Life on the Mississippi* and feel like him when I'm up there.

Our second houseboat.

Twain wrote of boys who dreamed of becoming riverboat pilots, and I dream along with them. The water is a realm all its own, an alternate reality flowing through the land-bound world. I may not have caught many fish, but the hook was set deep in me. My first book will feature a boy who runs off to sea. The same theme will form the core of the first tale in *Graven Images*. I'll fall in love with sailing, plying the waters of California and Maine on everything from dinghies to tall ships. The houseboat trips leave me with a yearning to see new places—an urge that never leaves.

Planning . . . or Not

If you've ever run out of room when writing "Happy Birthday" on a homemade card, then you know the value of outlines. They give you the big picture and keep you on track toward your goal. The longer the piece of writing, the more helpful they are. If you're fine with present pain in exchange for future happiness, outlines are for you.

Pain? Planning ahead means making your major story decisions up front. That's work. You'll need to walk through the story entirely in your head, figuring out which way to go at all the major forks in the road.

The payoff: when you start writing, you know just where you're headed, leaving you simply to put the story into words. You'll never find your main characters on the edge of a cliff and think, *I wonder how they're going to get out of this*? Nor will you need to delete the long scene you wrote to get them to the cliff in the first place. The more planning, the less rewriting.

So what's not to like about outlining? For many writers, it's too abstract, like eating a recipe for pizza instead of an actual slice. They'd rather plunge into the story and work out its problems on the ground instead of in the clouds. They might happen upon great lines and scenes they hadn't planned to write, discovering possibilities that never would have appeared in an outline. True, their first draft might be a mess, but now they know the best route to take—and they had a lot more fun finding it.

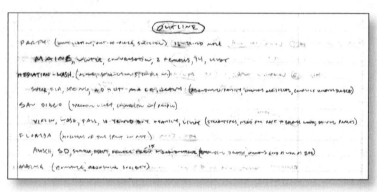

Outline of the novel Whirligig

My father belonged to this tribe. He rarely knew his endings beforehand and preferred to be as surprised as his readers. He trusted his imagination to get him out of any jams he'd written himself into.

I was a planner for most of my career. Figuring out an outline was essential for a complex book like *Whirligig*, in which present scenes alternate with future ones. But the older I've gotten, the more I've come around to my father's method. When you're improvising and things are falling into place, there's an excitement—nerve-wracking at times—that's addictive. I love maps, but as this book's title declares, you can have a great trip without them.

Which is best for you? Your own experience will guide you.

The stretch of coast beyond Santa Monica that beckoned

5
North

In that era before kids' soccer leagues and video games, my sisters and I entertain ourselves for hours going through people's trash. Archaeologists study garbage and we do the same courtesy of Santa Monica's alleys, where trash cans often stand out all week and are out of sight of their owners. What will we find? We never know. I also don't know the word *serendipity*—finding good things by accident—or how vital it is to artists of all sorts.

In our pharmacist neighbor's barrel, you might work your way through a deep layer of brochures about sleeping pills to find nothing more interesting than cat-food cans. But there was the red-letter day I found the gas mask two alleys over. And the baseball player's bat. And the collection of bombing maps of Germany from World War II, with the airplane's route plotted in pencil. And the working camera that I used for years. And the ten-dollar bill. The character Junkyard in *The Dunderheads* is highly autobiographical.

We revisit cans that have yielded exciting finds in the past. Once we're old enough to find our way home, all of Santa Monica is open to us. Mainly we get around by bicycle.

One day a neighborhood girl on a bike describes a discovery: an unsuspected canyon to the north, drained by a rushing river. She draws a map. Like the explorers of old, we're entranced by this vision. And so it begins.

My sisters and I follow the map, riding down, up, and down again into a neighborhood we've never seen. It's wooded, the houses strung along a narrow canyon. People probably speak English here, but we feel as if we're deep in Amazonia. We've abandoned trash hunting for pure exploration. We find the river. In truth, it's a spindly creek owing much of its flow to runoff from gardeners' hoses. We're thrilled nonetheless. Moving water has the same pull on us that gold has on prospectors.

We return repeatedly, mapping new routes. We discover that another steep climb will deliver us to an even more exotic realm: the ranch of Will Rogers. This actor and comedian, popular in the 1920s and 1930s, built a house there that included a stable and trails winding into the Santa Monica Mountains. The grounds also contain an immense grassy field where the locals entertain themselves with a bizarre game we've never seen: polo. Horses streak down the field, hooves thundering, their riders raising long-handled mallets and striking a wooden ball. We find one of the battered balls in the grass and bring it home as proof of the wonder we've beheld.

Inspired by the houseboat trip, I want to go farther. With the ocean on the west and Los Angeles to the south and east, the obvious direction is north. Southern California is freeways, smog, and concrete. Northern California, by contrast, is fog, ferns, and redwoods. The half of the state that lies beyond San Francisco is nearly all countryside. Like a compass needle, my thoughts point north.

During junior high, I begin pouring myself a bowl of cereal at night and opening the *Los Angeles Times* to the weather page. Weather barely exists in Santa Monica. I've never felt air colder than 45 degrees. My eyes search the page for northern cities. Halifax, Nova Scotia: high 4, low -17. The very look of those numbers makes me hungry to be there. Bangor, Maine: snow. Boston: freezing rain. Those luckies! Some hormone is urging me to plant myself among them, as far from home as possible.

My parents subscribe to *Sunset* magazine. Its stories about West Coast gardening and decorating hold no lure, but one day I discover the vacation ads in the back. I pore over the pictures of the Russian River, Cape Mendocino, the Skunk Train through the redwoods.

The shortwave has taught me how to send away for things. I write to the chambers of commerce and tourist boards that placed the ads. Soon, a new tributary begins flowing into my mail pile: maps and brochures covering the coastal counties up to

Oregon. Then all the way to British Columbia.

Canada exerts a powerful attraction. It's largely wilderness and closer than Alaska. Instead of trailer-filled campgrounds and tourist trains, Canada is raw nature. How to get there?

I enter high school, finally have a mild growth spurt, and move up to a green ten-speed Schwinn. It's got twin metal baskets on the back and an odometer on the front wheel that measures mileage. I begin riding farther up the coast, climbing up and then screaming back down Malibu's canyons. I love riding new roads.

One spring morning I'm in my front yard, standing over my bike. My friend Jeff is at the ready on his Raleigh. We're laughing as well as jittery. It's a Saturday morning, with Monday a holiday. Our parents have agreed to let us miss school on Tuesday and Wednesday. Like fairy-tale characters, we're about to set off into the wide world. We're headed north.

We careen down Santa Monica's 7th Street hill, gravity delivering us to Pacific Coast Highway. The light turns green and we make a right, heading up the coast. We've no inkling of the future trips that, like chess games, will all begin with this move.

I've tied a sleeping bag to my rear rack. The baskets on either side are half empty. A tent in case it rained? No need. Sixteen-year-olds are mad optimists. Water? A single metal canteen. Food? A few oranges. iPod and earbuds? Thirty years away; music for us is shelved in the brain. Entertainment means singing to yourself.

We pass Sunset Boulevard, then Malibu Pier at mile ten. I've made it this far in the past, but the ever-present need to head back home has kept me from riding farther. Not this time. The trip is truly on.

The plan is to ride round-trip to Isla Vista, one hundred miles away, where my older sister is in college. Bike touring is just getting started; we've seen the occasional long-distance biker but have never met anyone who's done it. We're making it up as we go along. The night before leaving, my father gave my bike a once-over, squeezed a tire, and wished us well.

We work our way over Malibu's hills, finally leave Los Angeles County behind, and enter a restaurant in Oxnard for a cold drink. I assured my parents we'd be safe with the words, "It's not like we'll run into the Hells Angels." Actually, members of the most notorious motorcycle gang in the land are walking out as we walk in.

We're in awe. So is the restaurant. When the bikers in black start up their Harley-Davidsons, the restaurant's entire population—probably stiff from pretending not to look at them—rushes to the windows to watch them go. I hope they'll head south. They turn to the north.

We follow, and reach Carpenteria. I look down at my odometer. We've ridden seventy-five miles. We're wildly impressed. Lacking social media, we share this news via the cutting-edge communications technology of the day: by feeding dimes into a pay phone and calling our friends one at a time.

By now it's late afternoon. Where will we sleep? We haven't thought that far. Planning is for travel agents.

Dinner is French bread smeared with cream cheese, eaten on the beach. Food has never tasted so good. As the only nearby campground is full, we pay eight dollars for a dingy motel room that features a fist-shaped hole in the wall. Wow. We feel like we're seeing real reality. Or at least a different corner of it from the one we'd see if we were traveling with our parents.

We've brought a copy of *Alfred Hitchcock's Mystery Magazine* to read aloud in the evenings. At roughly the same time, Jeff falls asleep listening and I fall asleep reading.

We cruise through Santa Barbara the next day, reach Isla Vista, and find my sister's apartment. Unfortunately, there isn't room for us to stay. No problem. To travel is to be open to chance. When we return to our bikes, Jeff's sleeping bag is gone.

Whoa. That's not chance—that's theft! We borrow my sister's bag and spend hours after dark searching for a safe place to sleep, finally choosing an unlit patch of grass near a road.

In the middle of the night comes the moment I've feared. I open my eyes to see two big men walking toward us. Hells Angels? Jeff is sleeping deeply. My mouth goes dry and I wait to experience my first fractured skull and/or armed robbery. Then they stop, aim a flashlight at us, and, miraculously, turn around.

I raise my head and realize they're driving off in a police car. They were probably checking to make sure we were alive. I understand why in the morning when I find we've been sleeping on a traffic island.

We retrace our way down the coast, making discoveries. Bananas don't really roast like marshmallows. Sleeping on sand is like sleeping on concrete. It's a bad idea to get separated from your trip partner if the cell phone hasn't yet been invented. We sweat up all those Malibu hills we flew down, then suddenly we're home, my odometer reading 235.

My friend Carrie presents us with a medal of honor: a piece of driftwood on which she's painted the word *Heroes*.

She's unaware that our trip will inspire her and three others to far outdo us. I, in turn, have no idea of the effect her trip will have upon me.

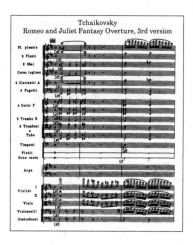

The first page of the score that my father brought home

6

Word Music

Some houses are steeped in religion, with a code of conduct, ritual objects, a special day of the week, and belief in a world beyond the one out the window. I grew up in such a house, except that religion was replaced by music.

Special day? Mondays, the day of my piano lesson with Miss Dixon.

Ritual objects? The small plaster busts of the great composers that Miss Dixon gives out, graven images I prize and line up on my windowsill.

Code of conduct? Wrists up. Practice the hard parts, not the easy ones. If the piece calls for B-flat, do not play B-natural from beginning to end, lest your mother rend her hair.

The separate reality? The tranquil meadows, eerie forests, and enchanting vistas built entirely of notes.

Everyone in my family plays an instrument. I play the piano in the living room. Beside it resides the classical guitar that my father practices in the evenings. My mother also plays the piano. Both my sisters play the flute. I'm awed by their ability to move their fingers correctly without ever looking at them. When they play duets, I wish I didn't play an instrument that's usually played alone by a single player.

In fifth grade, I get that chance, minus the instruments. My teacher announces that we'll be doing something new called *readers theater*. She hands everyone a set of stapled pages, the text of a play titled *The Bad Seed*. Roles are decided, and we starting reading our parts, with no need for makeup or sets.

The story catches us up at once, with its sugar-sweet girl our own age who murders a classmate and anyone else who thwarts her. When her mother finds out, and learns her own mother was a serial killer, she tries to kill her demonic child and then shoots herself. A teacher staging it today would be fired within minutes. We love it.

Beyond the story, I like the way that we all collaborate in performing it, as if we're an orchestra. Music and words are cousins. I notice when my father is reading his work aloud that there's a certain rhythm at the beginning of a chapter that goes with an opening. The sentences at the end somehow have the sound of an ending.

Several years later, my father takes up the alto recorder. I follow suit. I borrow his Trapp Family book and learn a new note or two each day until I've got most of them. Two school friends then recruit me to join them in a trio for two recorders and guitar. We perform the piece in our living room before family and friends. I'm nervous, my breathing uneven and fingers slippery with sweat, but I love being part of the group and hearing what results when our three lines are joined.

Synergy: when the whole is greater than the sum of its parts. I'm hooked from that day forward on chamber music.

How do composers hear all those lines in their heads? I find out when my father comes home from the library with the score of Tchaikovsky's *Romeo and Juliet* and shows it to my younger sister and me. We've never seen an orchestral score before, with the parts for all the instruments stacked on top of each other. My father lowers the needle onto our vinyl recording of the piece and we're off and running, following along on the score.

It's stirring music, the strings soaring with love, the cymbals portraying the clash of swords. The score shows how carefully it's put together. Some instruments are silent for long stretches until Tchaikovsky calls for them. You can see how he got a particular sound by combining a particular selection of instruments. It's part puzzle, part layer cake, with a thriller's driving plot.

Suddenly, I know what I want to do with my life. I want to write scores.

Just a few years earlier, Santa Monica Public Library made a momentous decision. Though *library* comes from *liber*, Latin for *book*, there was a move to admit records to the collection. Purists resisted, but the library ended up devoting a small room to vinyl recordings, complete with listening stations with headphones. I'm grateful they did.

With my library card, I work my way through Tchaikovsky's seven symphonies, then Beethoven's nine. Riding my bike to school, I hear Grieg's "Morning Mood" playing in my head. Brahms and Berlioz become the soundtrack to my high school romances.

My house is a musical smorgasbord, filled with the sounds of the Beatles, Broadway musicals, Herb Alpert and the Tijuana Brass, comedy, Vin Scully calling baseball, Joni Mitchell, flamenco guitar, Chopin waltzes.

I gradually realize I'm unlikely to perform any Chopin. I'm no piano prodigy. More like a B-minus student. I've been checking out biographies of composers, and they all seem to excel at playing instruments shortly after graduating from diapers. I'm also not sure I have the kind of brain that can hear twenty different lines at once. I check out books on harmony, but never study them seriously. My dream of composing suddenly looks half-baked.

I'm unaware that a bona fide composer, Ernst Toch, lives only a mile away. Driven out of Europe by the Nazis, he came to California and helped support himself by writing film music, including the score to *Heidi*—starring none other than Shirley Temple. One of his symphonies won the Pulitzer Prize, but his most popular piece is *Geographical Fugue*, a work for a chorus that doesn't sing but instead speaks place names. It's like a complicated round, with cities and countries instead of "Row, row, row your boat."

The opening of Geographical Fugue

My friend Bob hears *Geographical Fugue*. He writes a piece in the same style using names and phrases from the Bible. He needs three other speakers to perform it at an arts night at our high school. I'm one of them.

It's great fun to perform. Sometimes just one of us is speaking, sometimes all four talk over each other, staying always on the beat. Even though we're not singing or playing instruments, there's the exciting interplay of chamber music. As with Toch's piece, it's music made from words.

Then comes the day when I'm extra-specially grateful that records have been added to the public library—the day I check out *Under Milk Wood*. It's a word-portrait of a Welsh fishing town, written for radio by poet Dylan Thomas. He and five other speakers bring the place to life through dozens of characters, with humor and language richer than cream.

I find a book on Thomas and see a photo of the recording. The troupe is sitting on stools, their parts resting on music stands. No sets, costumes, or action. It's a play for voices. Another case of chamber music with words.

A shiver goes through me. I might not be able to

compose symphonies, but I feel like I could write word music. That shiver of excitement never leaves. It inspires many books, from the two-voiced poems in *Joyful Noise* to the multicharacter portrait of Los Angeles in *Breakout* to the autobiography of a radio-obsessed teen in *Seek*, told through a collage of fifty-two voices. Decades later, I'm still looking for new ways to re-create *Under Milk Wood*.

Brainstorming

There's a reason why "Where do you get your ideas?" is the question that writers hear most. People are mystified by the ability to put a book on the shelf that was never there before, to produce something out of nothing.

Ideas are underfoot everywhere, actually. The French writer Guy de Maupassant wrote one of the world's most famous short stories about a lowly piece of string. It's what you do with the idea that counts.

To turn one into a manuscript requires the writer's most important skill: brainstorming. Generating lines, characters, scenes, plots. Coming up with answers to questions that have no right answer. Why is he a recluse? Where did they meet? How did Lady Filbert escape the burning house even though she had two broken legs?

Because there's no right answer, you want a lot of possible answers. Just as with a restaurant menu, the more there is to choose from, the more likely you'll find something you like.

Coming up with answers can be tough. Here are my suggestions:

Write them down so you don't forget them.

Don't stop after the first one. Try to come up with a handful—or more.

Take short breaks.

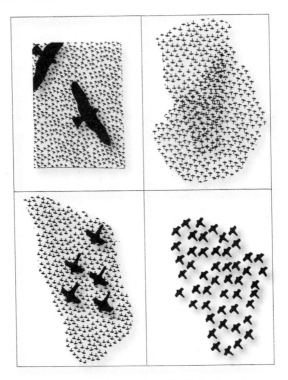

Some of my brainstorming with bird silhouettes

Consider combining answers.

When you get in a rut, keep asking yourself the question, *What could be different?*

One of the best ways to become a good brainstormer is to practice it in nonverbal spheres. I learned through art, starting in childhood, facing a blank page and deciding what to draw. The printing press gave me further practice. I'd consider lots of possible business-card designs before choosing the winner. I still work on art projects between books, coming up with variations on an idea, tweaking, combining, deciding. Any art form will hone your skills. These skills will transfer easily to writing. The more you use them, the better you'll get.

As inspiration, etch in your memory the statement reputedly made by the director of the U.S. Patent Office: "Everything that can be invented has been invented." Said to have been said in 1899. Your goal is to prove those words wrong, every minute.

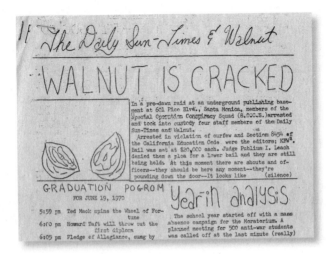

The Daily Sun-Times & Walnut

WALNUT IS CRACKED

In a pre-dawn raid at an underground publishing base-ment at 601 Pico Blvd., Santa Monica, members of the Special Operation Conspiracy Squad (S.O.C.S.) arrested and took into custody four staff members of the Daily Sun-Times and Walnut.

Arrested in violation of curfew and Section 8454 of the California Education Code. were the editors; KPW[2]. Bail was set at $20,000 each. Judge Publius I. Leach denied them a plea for a lower bail and they are still being held. At this moment there are shouts and of-ficers--they should be here any moment--they're pounding down the door--It looks like   (silence)

GRADUATION POGROM
FOR JUNE 19, 1970

5:59 pm Ted Mack spins the Wheel of For-tune
6:00 pm Howard Taft will throw out the first diploma
6:05 pm Pledge of Allegiance, sung by

year in analysis

The school year started off with a mass absence campaign for the Moratorium. A planned meeting for 500 anti-war students was called off at the last minute (really)

Page one of our last edition

7

The Daily Sun-Times and Walnut

"Your grandfather went to live with a tailor in another village when he was your age. To learn the trade."

The wrinkled great-aunt who's speaking seems impossibly old to my twelve-year-old self.

"There were three or four apprentices, all working for free. In exchange, the man was supposed to teach them, give them a place to sleep, and feed them. Only he forgot about the feeding part."

A breeze off the Pacific enters the living room, but we've all been transported to Russia in the time of the czars.

"So the apprentices got your grandfather to write a letter to someone, complaining. His reward? Being thrown into prison."

A doctor in the prison protected him. Somehow he got out, but Russia wasn't a safe place for Jews. His father decided it was time to leave. The pair of them set off on the six-hundred-mile walk to Hamburg.

"Crossing borders was the most dangerous part," says my great-aunt. "Soldiers with guns. It was night when they got to the border with Poland. They'd joined up with other emigrants, including a young mother. Her baby began to cry. She covered it with her shawl to muffle it. Then a blanket. They got across without the solidiers hearing them. Then the mother found out she'd smothered her baby."

This story is burned into my memory. I think of it when my mother teaches English in our home to immigrants now arriving from Latin America.

I'm much luckier than my grandfather in so many ways. For instance, when I'm sixteen, I'm able not only to lodge my complaints, but to circulate them through all of Santa Monica High School, courtesy of the school paper, *The Samohi*.

Taking journalism is a departure for me. Though my father had written for newspapers, I didn't see myself following in his footsteps any more than he'd wanted to sell clothing like his father. But then, in tenth grade, something happened. Something called *The Grapes of Wrath*, by John Steinbeck.

It wasn't a school assignment. It was just there, on the living-room table. I started reading. The next day I read more. I began looking forward to coming home and finding out what new troubles the Joad family had gotten into. Steinbeck hooked me not only on his characters, but on reading as a whole. From then on, I was never not reading a book.

I even take a slight interest in writing. In eleventh grade I have room for an elective and pick journalism. The class teaches us how to come up with interesting openings and how to avoid boring our readers with the word *said*.

"Threatening great bodily harm to encourage freshmen to shine the school seal is an ancient tradition," *noted* Principal Loony.

"Male students whose hair reaches their shoulders

will be given fifty lashes before the assembled student body," *commented* Vice Principal Flattop.

"Students who undermine school spirit by failing to attend pep rallies will be boiled in oil," *chirped* Dean Dareme.

We learn the strange alphabet of proofreading, with its symbols for inserting, deleting, and adding and subtracting space. We take a field trip to Santa Monica College, where the newspaper is printed. Then one day we're declared ready to write.

l.c.	Lower case--used in margin	⊓	Move up
/	Lower case--used in text	⊔	Move down
Caps.	Caps--used in margin	⊙	Insert period
≡	Caps--used in text	⋏	Insert comma
℘	Delete	;	Insert semicolon
⌒	Close up	:	Insert colon
⊋	Close up and delete	=/	Insert hyphen
W.f.	Wrong font	⌄	Insert apostrophe
‖	Align vertically	⌄⌄	Insert quotation marks
⊏	Move left	$\frac{1}{N}$	Insert 1-en dash
⊐	Move right	$\frac{1}{M}$	Insert 1-em dash

The symbols we learn before being issued our red pencils

I'm assigned to write features. The editor gives me the name of a girl in the senior class to interview.

"What should I ask her?"

"Ask her if she lives for the past, the present, or the future. It's what we always ask."

I find the girl, open my notebook, and ask her the question. She looks baffled. "I never thought about it."

I stare at her, desperate for an answer.

"A little for each, I guess," she says.

I sputter one or two further questions and write a brief feature. *"A little for each," she opined,* I type. My piece is so filled with air it's a miracle it doesn't float off the page. Apparently this quality is much sought after. In my senior year I'm promoted to features editor.

The Vietnam War is raging. The United States invades Cambodia and Laos. Most high school graduates who go on to college are exempt from being drafted; many of those who don't attend get swept into the war. Protests are widespread, as are inner-city riots, but you'd never guess any of this from reading *The Samohi*. One week, while Samohi graduates in Vietnam are dodging machine-gun fire, our editorial cautions against the dangers of running in the halls.

The disconnect is so huge that it can be seen from space. I ask our journalism teacher if I can write a satirical column that dares to mention the wider world. She agrees. I call the column "Humbug." My grandfather, recently dead, would be proud. He complained about hunger; I use humor to rant about President Nixon and the war.

After ten novels for adults, my father says he's received only two letters from readers, both pointing out typographical errors. But one day I get a postcard from someone in Santa Monica I don't know, an adult who's somehow gotten a copy of *The Samohi*, has read "Humbug" and taken the time to offer his compliments. I hadn't been aiming at readers beyond my classmates, but the idea of a wider audience laughing at my lines is an important encouragement. My taste for comedic commentary will later launch *Weslandia*, *The Dunderheads*, and *A Fate Totally Worse Than Death*.

Back when the San Diego newspaper my father worked for folded, he and some friends started their own tiny magazine to fill the gap. For once they could write whatever they wanted. That usually meant local news and political commentary, but for fun they once printed a photo of an alleged 27-inch alien that was said to have crash-landed in Mexico. The picture had come from a local flying saucer fanatic and was so obviously faked that they thought no one would take it seriously. Instead, the issue sold out and the story went national. They discovered the same thing we've discovered in our time—that much of the public can't tell facts from fiction. The magazine had a short life but was fun while it lasted.

The 27-inch man from the planet Etheria, as reported in Point *magazine*

I now find myself following in my father's footsteps again. Though it's fun writing "Humbug," the rest of the newspaper seems a lost cause, so two friends and I decide to produce our own. We each type up a single page. Joel's is called *The Free Samohi*. Jeff, my biking buddy, a transplant from Oregon, wittily names his *The Willamette Post-Nasal Drip*. I call mine *The Daily Sun-Times and Walnut*, claiming it's a Sunday supplement to the *Fresno Bee*.

Our material is wildly diverse: drawings, free ads, actual phone numbers to call for legal help next to an excerpt from the made-up memoir by Lydia Mayonnaise, fictional White House chef. "Two Southland Students Die in P.E. Action" vents our dislike for P.E. in the somber style of the *Los Angeles Times* war death announcements. We make copies, staple them, and hand them out to our friends.

The paper is a hit. We're famous. And infamous. The administration gets a copy and we're summoned to the first of many meetings with the dean of students. Distributing an unauthorized newspaper on school grounds turns out to be a violation of California's Education Code. We promise not to do it again.

A promise we break immediately. There's just too much to say. We settle on *The Daily Sun-Times and Walnut* and invite others to contribute. Pieces flow in. A sympathetic teacher slips us reams of paper, which we stash in an unused locker we've somehow gotten the combination to. In journalism class, where we're supposed to be working on *The Samohi*, we're typing *Walnut* stories on the big manual typewriters. Years later, our escapades will be transformed into Rob's pirate radio adventures in *Seek*.

Journalism class in the typewriter era, with Joel on the left and me on the right, probably working on the Walnut

We cover the move to legalize marijuana, other high schools' antiwar activities, the budding environmental movement, all with much mockery of

The Samohi. "Tall and lanky, small and quick, fat yet thin is Tim Wilson, non-athlete of the week," one of my pieces begins, parodying the style of *Samohi* features. We also make fun of Santa Monica's paper, the *Evening Outlook*, which lists its contents in a box titled "Your Outlook Inside." *The Walnut* begins including "Your Walnut Inside," which lists made-up stories not found in the issue and page numbers far higher than our usual four.

It's spring, and the winds of change are blowing. Under pressure, the administration revises the dress code. Girls can finally wear pants. To Jeff, the huge reproduction of Thomas Gainsborough's *The Blue Boy*, a classic from 1770 that hangs outside the library, is emblematic of our behind-the-times education. So he and some friends snip the wire holding it, take it to a car, and drive off. When no one seems to notice, *The Walnut* comes to the rescue, reporting on this heinous crime in a series of interviews with Mr. Art Robbers.

We also cover Skrugby, the soccer-with-an-eraser game we invented in seventh grade, the chosen sport of nerds. We use it to make fun of high school sports and the fervor devoted to football in *The Samohi*.

At the year's climactic Skrugby match, *The Blue Boy* is dramatically returned unharmed. Looking on, the vice principal clearly has no idea what to do with us.

Graduation approaches. *The Walnut* staff has big plans. We'll make our last issue look like a graduation program and distribute it from under our gowns.

We get to work. We write a parody graduation program for the cover. Inside, we offer a takeoff on "Dear Abby," the famous advice column; ours is "Dear Abbie," with questions answered by the political rabble-rouser Abbie Hoffman. We have poetry, actual college reports from previous year's graduates, and a year-in-review piece headlined to suggest the words *urine analysis*.

It's an eight-page production, our biggest by far. We lay it out, print it at a copy shop, and have a collating party. The next night, we break the California Education Code one last time. We put on our black gowns, pass stacks of copies to friends to give out, and circulate through the thousand-strong graduating class. We're doing this on campus, but what can they do to us now?

We're not arrested. No diplomas are withheld. The administration is no doubt overjoyed to see us go.

Was the issue a hit? I don't know, because suddenly high school is over.

The opening of Fruit Mélange

8

Berzerkeley

In September my parents drive me north to Berkeley, where I'll be at the University of California's oldest and most rebellious campus. The smoke from previous years' riots seems to hang in the air, just as their graffiti festoons walls.

Berkeley feels like a big city. One day I'm eating in a restaurant's courtyard when the word is passed from table to table: a man with a knife isn't letting anyone leave. In another few years, Patty Hearst will be kidnapped a few blocks away from where I live and begin a life of crime with the Symbionese Liberation Army. No wonder some people call it Berzerkeley.

I'm an English major. As requested, I'm reading Chaucer and Dickens, but college is a cafeteria of learning and I put a lot of other plates on my tray. I take botany and discover the world of plants that had been hiding in plain sight my whole life. I love my Latin class and for the first time understand how English grammar works.

I take many classes in music history. For one of them, I write a piece in the style of *Geographical Fugue*. It's scored for three speakers, each playing a percussion instrument. It begins with geography and then shifts to investment firms, fruit, bicycles, a quote from Hindu scripture, and more. It's a crazy mixture. Appropriately, I title it *Fruit Mélange*. It's never performed, but it's a vital first step on the road to *Joyful Noise*.

I've rarely been away from home. Though I get on well with my parents, I like being on my own in a place with different weather, new friends, a different vibe. Here the sun sets behind the Golden Gate or

Mount Tamalpais. We read the hilarious Art Hoppe in the *San Francisco Chronicle*. There's no texting back and forth with parents in this era; we write letters. Long-distance calls are seen as an expensive luxury, so I call home only twice a month. This is a boon, giving me plenty of room to lead my own life.

I have no idea where that life is headed and make stabs in various directions, with no one to tell me I shouldn't. I take astronomy and work up to being able to use the telescope in the university observatory. Learning the constellations leads me to learn the Greek myths behind them, leading to a lifelong interest in mythology and folklore.

I sit in on classes in criminology and linguistics. I apply to be one of the bell ringers in the Campanile, the campus's bell tower, where students use their hands, elbows, and feet on the waist-high wooden handles to produce chords. I'm not accepted, but put my feet to use in my folk-dancing class and become a regular at International House's packed dances. There, lines of students whiz past each other to music from Bulgaria, Sweden, Israel, Greece. The music is thrillingly foreign: instead of 4/4 rhythm, it might be in 7/8 or 11/16, featuring crusty relatives of the violin or bagpipes. I wake up in the morning with this music still in my head.

Ronald Reagan is governor of California and sees Berkeley as a hotbed of Marxism, but Thoreau is as much worshipped as Marx. Young people are founding communes at the ends of dirt roads and relearning the arts of growing food and building shelter. I take one of the school's first classes in ecology. One spring day I come home to find my roommate hunched over pieces of leather on the floor.

"Making some moccasins," he says in answer to my question.

He's true to his word. They go almost up to his knees. A day later he puts them on, dons a small pack, and sets off, spending the break between quarters tramping the bright green hills to the east. Another student I know is so entranced with the woods that he covers the floor of his room in leaves.

That summer I follow suit, living with a friend in a tent cabin on the Truckee River north of Lake Tahoe, trying to write down what I see: the feel of the sun's first rays, the flight of vultures, the view from the top of the trees I like climbing. I don't have a story to tell, but pure description seems a worthy goal and challenge. The future in which I'll describe birds and bugs in poems and write a biography of the naturalist John Townsend is too distant to glimpse. But I know that Thoreau filled thousands of pages with detailed notes on the natural world around him. And that Gary Snyder, a poet revered in Berkeley, spent years in the backcountry as a fire lookout and trail tender, keeping journals.

That contemplative life calls as my second year wears on. The university's quarter system compresses classes into a frantic rush. We read so many Shakespeare plays in so short a time that it's hard to keep the stabbings and poisonings straight.

I'm living in a student-filled rooming house with a big common kitchen. For the first time, I've had to learn to cook for myself. One resident delivers a passionate speech on the amount of time wasted on food preparation. One night I invite a girl to dinner and serve nothing but a baked yam. She hadn't heard the speech. She never returns.

I progress to making big batches of pea soup, stored in a collection of peanut-butter jars. As the freezer is always full, these go in the fridge. Eventually the soup begins to taste slightly sour.

Then conspicuously sour. Somehow it never makes me sick. A year later, my cast-iron stomach will come in handy.

The eating is better at the Heidelberg Restaurant, where I get my first job, busing tables and washing dishes. It's on Berkeley's main street, Telegraph Avenue, crowded as a bazaar with sellers of jewelry, Hare Krishnas tapping finger cymbals, chanters of poetry, political persuaders.

Berkeley's culture considers travel to be as viable a path to knowledge as study, an odyssey that teaches you about yourself and the world. Hitchhiking is regarded as travel's highest form, not just because it's free but because the reliance on chance connects you with the mysterious workings of the universe. The person who picks you up might become a lifelong friend or point you in an important direction. I hitched around the previous summer and came back with my head still attached to my body. Travel is calling me again.

Across the world, the Vietnam War is winding down. I'm no longer in danger of being drafted if I leave school. It's June. It's warm. For a Tolstoy class, I've read all 1,400 pages of *War and Peace*, not to mention *Anna Karenina* and the author's other major works. I'm hungry to leave the page behind and continue my education on the road. I've been saving my busboy money. Suddenly, my future becomes clear.

I'm not going to come back to Berkeley in the fall.

I'm going to use my money to buy a bicycle.

It's time to set off on my odyssey.

Using Your Own Life

Writers live for twenty-five years and spend the rest of their lives writing about it. Or so it often seems. Our families are the first worlds we know. The foods and attitudes served, the warmth and the warfare, the neighborhood and the times—this is the raw material most writers spin into books. But how?

You can capture it in memoirs. The alluring advantage: you don't need to invent. Your plot and cast have already been delivered to you. And readers love drama that's real, the reason we have reality TV and "based on a true story" on movie credits.

There are disadvantages here as well. Life isn't a perfectly plotted book. It might contain long stretches where nothing much happens. The cast of characters you've been dealt might not be that interesting.

And then there's the problem of unsustainability.

The first book almost always uses the author's best material. Sequels tend to be less and less compelling. Memoir writers can easily find themselves out of material, retreading their youth or reporting on their book tours.

But instead of simply writing down the facts of your life, you can alter, as fiction writers do. My grandfather's coming to America was one of the inspirations behind *Seedfolks*, with its focus on immigration, but everything in his story was changed. He arrived around 1900, but the book takes place in the present. He planted himself in New York; *Seedfolks* takes place in Cleveland. It has no characters from Russia. There's no smothered baby.

Fictionalizing turns our limited lives into renewable resources. By altering material in different ways, you can write book after book about the same experience. When my first wife and I adopted two brothers from Mexico, the theme of immigration reentered my life in a major way. I wanted to write about it without repeating *Seedfolks*. Fiction makes that possible. *The Matchbox Diary* is a picture book rather than a novel, one that's focused on one kid instead of a large cast, set in the past rather than the present. Is he from Mexico? No—Italy.

There are degrees of disguise. You could just change the names of the people around you, risking their wrath when they recognize themselves. The more you leave strict autobiography behind, the freer you are to create more satisfying stories. I attached some of my traveling experiences to Brent in *Whirligig* but gave him a motive and personality that weren't mine at all. I turn males into females, old into young, and have even crossed the border into other creatures. The poems in

My sons after becoming citizens

Joyful Noise are about insects, but many of the themes are straight out of my life.

Recasting that material isn't always easy. Invention and decision-making are required. See my advice on brainstorming and planning.

My route from sea to shining sea

9
The New World

I return to Santa Monica, buy a better bike, and call up my friend Kenyon. "Interested in another trip?"

Two summers after my high school bike trip, my friend Carrie, along with two other girls and a guy, built big-time on our discovery that serious miles could be covered by bike. Getting a ride with their bikes up to Vancouver, they proceeded to cross—with occasional hitching and assists from the train—the entire width of Canada, all the way to Halifax, Nova Scotia. Kenyon was on that trip. They sent postcards describing thunderstorms, the Calgary Stampede, swimming to islands in lakes, taking ferries. I was madly envious. Now it's my turn to lead the troops out.

The plan is vague: ride to Vancouver, then take a vote. Kenyon says yes. I've already signed up a Berkeley friend and her sister, who'll join us when we reach the Bay Area. In late June, Kenyon and I get a ride to Santa Barbara—we've already ridden that stretch—and set off the next morning.

The trip begins eerily. There aren't any campgrounds nearby when the sun gets low on our first day, so we bed down in some woods off Highway 1. I bolt up in the night, awakened by high-pitched screeching. Something is in the woods with us. Then I hear screams. First from animals, then from humans. Kenyon is in dreamland, but my heart is pounding. I grab my pocketknife just in case. The screeching finally stops. It takes an hour before I get back to sleep. In the morning we emerge from the trees, start riding, and see that just around the bend is a drive-in theater. What's playing? *Ben*, a horror movie about an army of trained rats.

Moral: always check the movie listings.

Actual moral: no guidebook on Earth reminds bikers not to camp near drive-ins. Dealing with what comes is all you can do.

We make it to the rugged stretch of coast known as Big Sur. A sign warns us: HILLS AND CURVES. Below that is the additional message: NEXT 63 MILES. The signs don't lie. The cliffs are high, the views stunning, and the close calls many when we're passed by supersized RVs. When we reach the sisters' home in Palo Alto, their father spares us the dangers of Bay Area traffic and gives us a lift over the Golden Gate. We get off in Marin County and head up the coast.

We're pointed north, but the wind is pointed south. Powerfully so. In the afternoon it makes for constant static in our ears, not to mention forcing us to actually pedal when we should be coasting downhill. The injustice! Unfortunately, we want to see Canada, not San Diego.

A typical day begins with us drenched in dew. Making oatmeal over a fire in a campground. Leaving early before the wind wakes up, the cool air scented with sea and sage. Stopping to pick blackberries. Going into a store to buy a can of soup for dinner. Finding a campground. Possibly being offered pie and ice cream by campers motivated either by respect or pity. At night I write anything notable that happened in the little notebook I've brought. When we hit the Eel River redwoods, we sleep with our heads around the vast trunk of the same tree, the thick mattress of dried leaves wonderfully springy.

We cross into Oregon. We're so glad to be done with our home state's hills that we burn our California maps that night. We don't realize that the hills in Oregon are a little bit bigger. Or that a day later our merry band will be radically reorganized.

Kenyon's already been to Vancouver and across Canada. He decides to turn back and fly home. I'm not as close to the sisters and miss his presence. When we three share a campsite with a group of male northbound bikers, I arrange a marriage. The sisters agree to join the guys, and I'll go on by myself.

Up the coast I go, over the Rogue River, sending my father a postcard from Humbug Mountain State Park. I wanted to be alone, but now miss companionship. One afternoon I ride into an Oregon campground and spot a friendly looking couple whose picnic table sports a jar of wildflowers. I stroll over and we end up eating dinner together. They're in a car, making a loop around the country from the east coast. We exchange addresses in the morning.

The Columbia River is so wide at its mouth and the wind so strong that it feels like it takes me an hour to cross the bridge. I enter Washington and am awed, days later, by the sight of Mount Rainier looming over the land as I ride the ferry into Seattle.

A week later I'm waiting in the Vancouver train station. It's easy to take a vote when there's only one of you. I've decided to turn east, but I can't see repeating my friends' ride. Unlike them, I pedaled to Vancouver and figure the 1,400 miles into the wind has earned me a train trip across Canada. I buy a ticket all the way to the east coast. What will I do when I get off the train? I have no idea.

It'll take four days and nights to get there. I break up the trip by getting off for three days in Jasper in the Canadian Rockies. I ask about the milky-gray Athabasca River and am told the color comes from particles of rock ground up by the glacier at the river's source. I'm truly in the North at last.

The Athabasca River flowing through Jasper National Park

Man doesn't live by food alone. I've brought enough bread, peanut butter, honey, and bananas to get me across Canada, but I run out of reading material in Manitoba. When the train makes a quick stop in Winnipeg, I dash into the station, search frantically for a book, and run out with a paperback called *Beyond Your Doorstep*. It contains nature writer Hal Borland's observations of the woods and meadows of his rural corner of Connecticut. It's full of nor'easters and spring peepers and woodchucks and other things I've never seen—the world my train is clacking toward. I read it all the way across Ontario.

I stretch my legs when we stop in Ottawa and notice something strange about the air. Then I realize: this is the humidity I've heard about but never felt. I'm in a new world.

Montreal. Quebec City. Then along the St. Lawrence and across the Gaspé Peninsula to the small town printed on my ticket: Matapédia. Amazingly, my bike is still there in the baggage car. The porter lifts it down, I pedal east, and behold the Atlantic for the first time. I can hardly believe it. Or the fact that the girl tending a blueberry stand speaks no English but only French. We laugh and make do.

The next morning I see the sun rise out of the water instead of set into it. I must really be on the other side of the continent. I take the ferry to Prince Edward Island, with its tidy towns and rolling corn-fields, and do my laundry there for only the second time on the trip, putting 98 percent of my clothes into the laundromat's washer. On to Nova Scotia, where I salute the four friends who came to Halifax before me. In New Brunswick, I camp alongside the

Bay of Fundy and see it do its magic trick from the first row; the water is gone in the morning. I ride down the coast of Maine and make it to Boston.

My friends had to fly back from the east and start college, but I'm free to stay. I decide to do exactly that. But where? It's September now, time to get settled before winter arrives.

I check out Northampton, Massachusetts, where a Berkeley friend is living, but I want someplace more rural. I ride north up the Connecticut River Valley, where fields are turning gold and tobacco is drying in sheds. From out of my saddlebag I pull the address of the couple I'd met back in Oregon. They're in southern New Hampshire. I head toward their town, Henniker. I find their road, then their house.

I arrive a day before they do. The door is opened by the house's owner, a woman who's wary but invites me in. I notice a piano. On its stand is the identical music that was on our piano in Santa Monica when I left—the Bach sonatas for flute and piano. She turns out to play the flute. I accompany her on one of the movements and all worries are erased. We're citizens of the same realm.

David and Jennifer show up the next day and feel like instant friends. I'll need a job. They point me toward New England College, where I'm hired to work in the kitchen. My dishwashing résumé is becoming impressive.

One of the other dishwashers is looking for a roommate to share a house. It's out in the country. I take a look. It's white with green shutters and dates from 1770. It has a barn and a field lined with sugar maples. There's no phone, electricity, or hot water, but after camping for months it's a step up in amenities.

I say yes. The trip that will be transformed into Brent's bus tour in *Whirligig* is finally over. I take the saddlebags off my bike. My odometer for the trip reads 2,350. I'm finally home.

My New Hampshire house

10

Back to the Future

My housemate, Neil, and I are caretaking the house for its Boston owner. Our sole obligation is to fire up the gas mower and crop the field to keep the woods from reclaiming it, something we never do. Since we pay no rent, I only need to work part-time, leaving me plenty of opportunity to explore.

We're at the end of a dirt road. Beyond the house I find a stunted apple orchard amid the forest. I stumble upon—and almost into—cellar holes. Rock walls wander through the woods. All are signs of a vanished world, back when New Hampshire was cleared and covered with farms instead of forests. The past is palpable here.

We live a modified eighteenth-century lifestyle. For light, we use kerosene lamps. For heat, we have a fireplace and an oil-burning heater, then later a wood stove. A creek behind the house provides the water flowing out of the kitchen tap. My Berkeley pea soup protects me from ills arising from our lack of a refrigerator.

There's no clock in the house. During one stretch I lose track of time and show up at a birthday party a day early. But we get twentieth-century help from the laundromat in Henniker and from friends with showers. We also buy batteries for our radio as often as other people buy milk. The announcers on WBCN and WGBH come to feel like close friends.

I've never lived in the country or in a place with real winter. Or in woods, which I've never liked. When the bike trip took me away from the ocean and into the trees for a few days, I always felt uneasy. Everything around me now is new. I begin making the strange familiar.

I buy one of the small Golden Nature Guides on birds. There inside is the jay I've been seeing, with its striking, stage-makeup markings, so different from the jays in the West. That cheery flitterer among the branches is a chickadee. Insect-seeking nuthatches move down tree trunks; creepers move up. Knowing their names makes the woods feel less foreign.

When I hear a bird I don't know, I take off in that direction, getting as close as I can and trying to remember everything I see. Straight tail or notched? Bill thick or thin, straight or curved? Like my aunt, I write down what I see in a notebook.

I do the same with trees. I find I'm living among beeches, birches, black walnut, ash. The thin maples turning crimson at the edge of lakes and marshes turn out to be red maples. This is the first forest I've known. Forever after, the deciduous eastern woods feel like the model for what woods should be.

I come to enjoy walking through the woods to get to the road where I hitchhike to work. I read in a book how lichens make a start on bare rock, create a little soil that's sufficient for mosses, then the mosses pave the way for flowering plants. I'm doing the same: starting from scratch.

This new life holds new people. Neil is an artist who can play any musical instrument you can point at. He introduces me to jazz. When I walk home late at night and hear strange chords coming from our house, I seem to be in that part of a horror movie when the audience shouts "Turn around!"—but it's just Neil playing the house's pump organ.

David is wise in country ways and shows me how to cut a sapling, climb on the roof, and use it as a chimney brush. He teaches me how to split wood. Through him I meet Peter, who stages musicals at New England College and will one day have a major hand in *Wicked*. He in turn points me toward the college's recorder consort, which I join. Here I meet Vicki, with whom I play duets for hours. It's pure pleasure. A decade later I'll try to give others the same joy via the poetic duets about birds in *I Am Phoenix* and then again in *Joyful Noise*.

The recorder consort is the first formal musical group I've been part of. We play everything from Renaissance dances to pieces by composers who are still in good health. I learn to play the bass recorder and like hearing the music from this basement vantage. Marilyn Ziffrin is our director and a composer as well. Bundling into her huge station wagon with its distinctive bumper sticker—I LOVE TUBAS— we play in women's clubs and town halls in New Hampshire and Vermont. Marilyn knows I've arrived with just the clothes on my back and kindly rents a black suit for me to wear at our big end-of-year concert. Rubber overshoes, alas, are my only black footwear.

There's no folk dancing here. Instead, there's contra dancing, just as described at the end of *Whirligig*. What better place for Brent to reengage with society? Picture a square dance stretched into a rectangle, with long lines of couples instructed by a caller and a live band playing Celtic tunes. It's fast and festive, pulling people out of the woods like a magnet. There's a potluck at the halfway point and a waltz at the end. Bands and callers rotate from town to town. I begin picking up the schedule and going with my new friends.

Fall is fabulous. Tourists drive north for hours to feast on the colors, but I live surrounded by them. My first winter is an even greater revelation. I experience snow in its ideal setting: brushing softly against the window of a warm house at the end of a road. The house has a pair of snowshoes. I realize I can snow-shoe as far as I want through the woods and simply follow my prints home, with no fear of getting lost. With the bugs gone and marshes frozen, I can walk out to places I could never get to before. The snow is printed with an alluring catalog of tracks.

Clear days are the coldest. I buy the Golden Nature Guide on weather. When a front is passing and the wind is blowing thirty miles an hour, I learn everything I need to know about wind chill. One day after leaving a friend's where I've showered, I touch my hair and realize it's frozen in place.

Others lose power, but we have no power to lose. Self-sufficiency feels good. We cook on a kerosene stove in the frigid kitchen. The outhouse, reached through the woodshed, is even colder.

Clear winter nights are the best time for star watching. Walking home in the dark, it's a comfort to look up at the strip of sky between the trees and recognize the constellations. Some nights I put on my wool peacoat and the rest of the winter clothes I've acquired, rush outside, look up at the region

I'm studying, then hurry back in to warmth and my star map. Some lucky souls see the northern lights.

Winter is long. In Henniker's grocery, the vegetable offerings shrink to onions, carrots, and potatoes, the rest of the case covered with brown paper. During thaws, the melting snow and icicles on my roof make it sound as if we live under a waterfall.

When spring finally comes, students stand outside in the sun and joyfully kick a soccer ball high over Henniker's main intersection. The nighttime chorus of frogs and crickets is deafening. The entrancing sight of fireflies plants a seed that will come up later in a poem for two voices.

Sap is on the move. I read about making maple syrup, buy taps at the hardware store, and pound them into the sugar maples by the house. The clear liquid drips into empty cans I've brought home from the New England College kitchen. One afternoon I boil it down. It takes forty gallons of sap to get one of syrup. This takes time. I don't finish until the middle of the night, the sugary cloud rising into my drowsy face as I stir. In the morning there's an extra surprise: the syrup left in the pan has turned to maple sugar. Precious treasure.

I'm not the only one who's entered a new world. My sister Jane visits on her way home from Ireland, where she's been working as a nanny. Her accent is so thick I can barely understand her. My sister Anne will shortly move to Jerusalem, where she'll operate entirely in Hebrew. It's a time for trying new identities.

When David and Jennifer marry in May, Peter and I play our recorders at the wedding. There's an outdoor contra dance afterward. It's blackfly season, causing much of the guest list to give off the acrid smell of Woodsman Fly Dope. But with Dudley Laufman, the contra-dance king of New Hampshire, calling and playing accordion, a fine time is had.

Summer comes around again, the woods echoing with the hermit thrush's flutelike call. I can't believe how dramatic a backdrop the seasons are here. All was white just a few months ago; now the world is green. In Santa Monica, I used to get March and May mixed up. Not here.

FIREFLIES ∞∞∞∞∞∞∞∞∞∞∞∞∞∞∞∞∞∞∞∞∞∞∞∞∞∞∞∞∞∞∞

Light	Light
	is the ink we use
Night	Night
is our parchment	
	We're
	fireflies
fireflies	flickering
flitting	
	flashing
fireflies	
glimmering	fireflies
	gleaming
glowing	
Insect calligraphers	Insect calligraphers
practicing penmanship	
	copying sentences
Six-legged scribblers	Six-legged scribblers
of vanishing messages,	
	fleeting graffiti
Fine artists in flight	Fine artists in flight
adding dabs of light	
	bright brush strokes

Signing the June nights	Signing the June nights
as if they were paintings	as if they were paintings
	We're
flickering	fireflies
fireflies	flickering
fireflies.	fireflies.

~~~~~~

It's eight miles from my house to Henniker. If I'm hitchhiking rather than biking, I look around while I wait for a ride, gather weed stems and sticks, make holes in wood with my knife's awl blade, and build little constructions. I've always made such "found sculptures" from ingredients supplied by chance. But one day the car that picks me up is driven by a real carpenter. Out of need, not the workmanship of the leaning tower of twigs I've made, Hector offers me a job.

I got a well-deserved C in seventh-grade wood-shop, but Hector teaches me how to use the tools of the trade. Over the fall and spring, he, Neil, and I build a house from the foundation up.

I could never see exactly how my father built his books, but here everything's visible. We raise the studs that will be walls, run the wires and pipes that will be hidden from sight. I learn a ton. Hector calls us his girls because our hair is long, so I buy us name tags reading FAYE and ANITA. When he's gone, we tune the radio to WBCN and dance through the unfinished house to "Spirit in the Night" by a new-comer to the rock scene named Bruce Springsteen.

Neil spends months at a time in Boston. In need of companionship, I happily take in a stray dog, the first of many canines in my life.

My father on a visit

Sometimes I jot things in a notebook:

The leaves sail to the ground, finally meeting
their shadows
Old Sizzlebritches: a name for the devil
A choir of candles
Book idea: Imaginary Birds of Eastern
North America

In a few years my house in the woods will be transformed into the one at the center of *The Half-a-Moon Inn.* Some people find living where I do to be spooky, especially when I tell them that the Arabic words on our mailbox mean *Castle of Blood.* The explanation: our Boston landlord's father, who used to summer here, was a chemist whose work on blood took him to the Middle East, where he studied the blood types of mummies.

His books are on our shelves and speak of wide interests. I have lots of time to read, and draw heavily from his library. When I pull William Shirer's *The Rise and Fall of the Third Reich* off a shelf, I realize how little I know about my own time, not to mention the centuries before. I never took a history class at Berkeley.

And yet history, like nature, is all around me.

Close by the house, on a rise surrounded by a rock wall, is a small cemetery used by the house's earlier occupants. I've gone there often. The gravestones go back to the 1830s. The first names come from the Old Testament: Benjamin, Rachel, Jacob, Sarah. There are more than a few shin-high stones marking infants' graves.

The cemetery

One day when I'm there, it hits me that I'm waking up in the same bedroom that many of these people awoke in. I'm taking water from the same creek.

Hearing the same birds. Walking up the same hill to the house. A chill of connection passes through me. And suddenly, in the midst of looking toward the past, I can see a new stretch of my future. After two years, I'm ready to return to school.

This time, college won't be the default choice, as it was for my friends and me after high school. And I won't be studying English or music. This time I'll study history.

Rock, lichen, moss, ferns, violets . . . I've so liked this process that I want to do it again, moving to some new part of the world. But where?

Serendipity supplies the answer. It brought me to David and Jennifer's campsite. Then to Henniker. Then to Neil, who's told me tales of living in a corner of the country that was as hard for me to picture as New England had been. It sounds perfect.

I start packing.

Practicing

A pro golfer's bag contains fourteen different clubs for different situations. A writer carries just as many. We need to know how to invent plots, create characters, do research, craft dialog that sounds real, and write description that lets readers see what we want them to see.

Athletes practice constantly. Here are a few ideas for writing practice that will build literary strength and agility.

Brainstorming

Try inventing ten new handshakes with a friend. Design twenty new alphabet letters. Draw thirty different versions of capital A. Come up with a logo built out of your initials. Construct a found sculpture with your plate and silverware and other kitchen-table ingredients.

Characters

Writers need characters who are both compelling and plausible. Try to meet those two tests when inventing a past for a character who collects snow globes. Someone who sets an extra place at the table that's never occupied. A person whose bedroom light goes on each night at three a.m. A character who gives out something other than candy on Halloween.

The first page of Seedfolks, *proof that writing never comes out right the first time*

Description

Similes and metaphors make words come alive. "He could take a bath in a shotgun barrel" beats "He was really skinny" by a mile. See if you can come up with something as good for a character who's a deep sleeper. Or a fast talker. Or an off-key singer. Or a loud laugher.

Plotting

A city kid wants a llama for a pet. You'll need a believable reason why. And obstacles to overcome. (Does she live in a high-rise?) And clever solutions to the obstacles that won't have popped immediately into readers' minds. Add to the mix other characters who help or hinder the quest. Go for it.

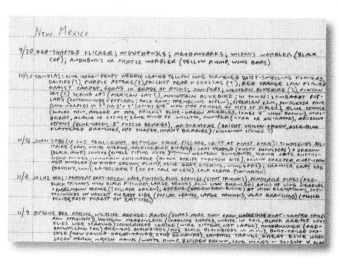
Bird notes I made soon after arriving in New Mexico

11
A Fork in the Road

It's a fall day, spitting rain, and I'm riding a city bus from Albuquerque's airport. I've just landed in a state I've never seen, where I have no family or friends or acquaintances.

Anxiety-producing, but exciting.

The couple behind me is speaking Spanish. We pass a store advertising itself as a panaderia. What's that? I feel like a spy dropped into a strange country, except that I haven't been briefed. I wonder where to get off. I spot a cheap motel, pull the cord, and work my hundred-pound suitcase off the bus. I check into a room, lie back on the bed, and open my newspaper to the classifieds. I need a place to live.

Police cars converge on the bar across the street. My neighborhood seems to merit the bars on the windows, quickening my search. I open my map. I see that the Rio Grande runs north-south, as do the imposing Sandia Mountains on the city's eastern border. The University of New Mexico, which I hope to attend, lies between them.

Checking out apartments on foot over the next days, I also check out New Mexican food. I've never tasted sopapillas or posole. Immigrants to America in my grandfather's era, who'd never seen a banana, sometimes bit right into the skin; I do the same with my first tamale, unaware that the corn husk around it isn't part of the meal.

I hear the question "Red or green?" a lot. This refers to chile sauce. The scent coming down the block is from green chiles being roasted in a rotating drum in front of a produce store. The aroma is captivating. No wonder the state's motto is the Land of Enchantment. I'm in another new world.

I find a room in a house and haul my suitcase two miles across town, with many stops to rest. Wheeled luggage has not been invented. The landlord has crudely divided the house's living room with a wall down the middle. I'm in one half and can conveniently converse with my neighbor through the gaps. Amazingly, he never complains when I bring home a portable stereo and begin a long journey through operas, masses, and the rest of the classical vocal catalog that I've never listened to. Either he's deaf or he likes Verdi.

I find work as a dishwasher, of course. Then again, George Orwell relied on the same trade and wrote a book about it—*Down and Out in Paris and London*. I check it out with my new Albuquerque Public Library card. I find new friends in the local folk-dancing scene.

I don't own a car but explore the area by joining Audubon Society outings that use carpools. Instead of mosses and ferns, I'm in the land of cholla cactus and piñon pine. I see roadrunners scurry and tarantulas migrate.

Whereas every house in New England seemed to have a copy of *Walden*, here the book is *Bless Me,*

Ultima, the New Mexican coming-of-age story by Rudolfo Anaya. He teaches at the university. Santa Fe's famed outdoor opera house is just an hour away. Painters and photographers abound. I've landed on rich soil.

The university admits me and I start classes in January. Being in school this time feels different. I know just what I want. I was a dutiful student before; now I'm driven.

I have a lot of catching up to do in history. New Mexico is a great place to do it. The Puritans reached Plymouth Rock in 1620, Jamestown got its start in 1607, but the Spanish established their New Mexican capital in 1598. A mall is named for Coronado, who was here in the flesh in 1540, searching for the fabled Seven Cities of Gold. The Puebloans, Navajos, Hopi, and other indigenous cultures who preceded the Europeans are still very much present.

The city is roughly half Hispanic. English speakers are latecomers here. It's the first time I've lived in a place where white people aren't the overwhelming majority. Here, we're called Anglos.

My boss at the restaurant is a Texan, part of

the latest invasion. Invaders are seldom welcomed. IF GOD WANTED TEXANS TO SKI, HE'D HAVE GIVEN THEM A MOUNTAIN, says a bumper sticker. My boss is tall, blond, and ornery. He once shuts me in the dark of the refrigerated storage room, leaving me to feel my way to the light switch. I'm not disappointed, months after I leave, when his restaurant blows up in the middle of the night.

I take American history, the history of the ancient Greeks and Romans, American social history, the history of the Far East. On my own, I study folklore and mythology, pulled by something primal. Perhaps it's their tales of heroic quests, since I'm still searching for my own place in the world.

I'm apprehensive about the heat my first summer. It is indeed hot, but I like the afternoon thunderstorms, the chorus of cicadas, and swimming in the Rio Grande with friends. We walk the network of irrigation ditches and visit butte-top Acoma and the Puebloans' other villages. We explore northern New Mexico, where families proudly consider themselves Spanish and the narrow fields hark back to medieval Europe. Older still are the Salmon Ruins, where my new archaeologist friend, Nancy, is working on a

Pueblo site dating from 1100. Old worlds within this new world.

It's a little-known realm for many. I discover the column in *New Mexico* magazine called "One of Our 50 Is Missing," with accounts of tourists inquiring about passport requirements when visiting New Mexico, what currency to bring, what voltage is in use. Many Americans think they're coming to a foreign country.

In some ways they are. The smell of piñon pine smoke, the taste of green chile stew and Indian fry bread, the long flat-topped mesas: it's not like anywhere else in the U.S. South of Albuquerque, my friends and I camp in the Manzanos, the range's gradual rise from the Rio Grande valley unmarked by any sign of human habitation. They must look just as they did when Coronado saw them. It's easy to lose track of the centuries here.

Albuquerque is a port city without water, attracting immigrants from all over. My housemate, Wanda, drawn west from Maryland, was a caretaker for Georgia O'Keeffe, the celebrated painter who herself was pulled from New York by northern New Mexico's landscapes. Wanda leads us north often, points out Pedernal, the peak O'Keeffe painted repeatedly, but we refrain from knocking on the famous woman's door. Her adobe house has a central atrium to bring in the light an artist needs. Somewhere within, she's painting.

I finish my first year, then another. My plan has been to go to graduate school in history, but suddenly I'm not so sure. I wonder if the scholarly life is really the one for me. I shift to Plan B: teaching history at a high school. This requires taking education classes after graduation and getting a credential. Two things happen on the way to this goal: I read a book and I hear a song.

The book is Bernard Malamud's novel *The Fixer*. It's based on the true story of a Russian Jew accused of killing a Christian boy to use his blood in making Passover bread, the hot fake-news claim of its time. The man is imprisoned in solitary confinement. When someone is put in the neighboring cell, the two attempt a desperate coded communication by pounding on the thick wall with their wooden shoes. One day, there's no reply. The neighbor turns out to have hung himself. The main character is crushed, and so was I. I find his isolation unbearable. Maybe my identification comes from my grandfather's prison experience in Russia. Suddenly, I know something new and important, that I have the character's same need to be heard and that this will be central to my life.

In this moment, mute Aaron at the center of *The Half-a-Moon Inn* is born. I'll begin writing the book within a year. I also realize that the audience I want to connect to is larger than a classroom of thirty students.

As if to create as many lines of communication with the outside world as possible, I sign up for classes in French and German, taught in the same room, one right after the other. I've already been studying Spanish on my own. Later I'll add sign language.

To accommodate this new drive, I switch from history to a general major that gives me more latitude. Graduation inches closer. I hear grim reports from others about education classes. I'm caught in a whirlpool of doubt.

If I'm not going to teach, how am I going to make a living?

I could write. This would satisfy my compulsion to communicate, but what do I have worth saying?

Though I've continued adding bits and pieces to my writing notebook, I haven't built up to whole stories. I seem to suffer from the most crippling obstacle a writer can have: a cloudless youth. Where's the well of tragedy and hurt that will fill my pen?

One night I see a performance of Leonard Bernstein's *Candide*, a brief opera based on Voltaire's classic. When the two main characters, about to wed, sing a duet picturing their future happiness, I notice something. The woman seated in front of me is crying.

Suddenly, I see a way out of my predicament. A way that takes me back to Radio Biafra on my shortwave and opens a route to the rest of my life.

We respond to universal emotions, I realize. Love, in the case of the *Candide* duet. Fear, in the case of Radio Biafra. We all know these and a hundred other feelings. We all grapple with separating from our parents, finding a meaningful role in the world, finding love. No searing tragedy or decade in rehab is required to access these. Every life has more than enough material. Even mine.

Knowing my predicament, my father suggests

I might want to test out the literary life by writing something short for young readers. Though I'd wanted a realm separate from his, I wonder if he might be on to something. Maybe music and history were meant to be sidelights, not my main endeavor. Maybe writing was meant to be my life's work.

I go home to Santa Monica at Christmas and write a story called *The Birthday Tree*. I've always heard that the tree in front of our house was planted to celebrate the birth of a child born to earlier residents. I mix that germ with the universal story of a boy leaving home for the first time. I draw on my love of birds and make up what sound like motifs from folklore: a seagull perched in the tree is a sign to the parents that their son is traveling over water; a meadowlark means he's traveling over land.

I show the piece to my father. He's highly complimentary. He also has suggestions. I come to realize that I've only written a first draft. A second follows. A third. A fourth. A fifth.

Eventually he thinks it's polished enough to send to his agent, who sends it on to Charlotte Zolotow, the esteemed editor at Harper & Row. A few weeks later I get word that she wants to publish it.

```
            THE BIRTHDAY TREE


        Once there was a sailor who fled from the sea.  He
   and his wife, who had lost three sons to the deeps, gathered
   up their belongings in a creaky wheelbarrow and left the
   water behind them.
        "A plague on the sea," said the sailor to his wife.
   "It whistles a sweet tune to lure the boys out of the hills
   and down to the boats.  But it pipes other tunes as well --
   shrieking winds and ships splitting on rocks."
        At nightfall the sailor cupped his hands to his ears.
   He could no longer hear the sea.
        After another day's walk the sailor took out his
   spyglass.  He could no longer glimpse the sea.
        On the third day the sailor and his wife found them-
   selves in a green valley.  They could no longer smell the sea.
        "It's here we'll put down," said the sailor.
```

The final draft of The Birthday Tree

The news seems too good to be true. My girlfriend, Becky, and I celebrate with green chile enchiladas that leave our lips buzzing.

It's been a long road. A winding one. A great one. One that opens onto further new roads.

I start thinking about what to write next.

Building a found sculpture on the California coast

12

Flash-Forwards

Becky became my first wife. Charlotte Zolotow became my longtime editor, a partner in literary excursions that would take me into novels, poetry, biography, and beyond.

I found I needn't have worried about following in my father's footsteps. We might both be writers for children, but we each had our own territory— his books aimed at middle graders, mine geared to teens and new readers. When he won the Newbery

Medal for *The Whipping Boy* in 1987, I couldn't have been more exultant. When *Joyful Noise* won two years later, he felt the same.

Athletes know the benefits of cross-training: it adds other sports' strengths and skills to your repertoire. For me, cross-training was my main training. I never took a class in writing or read a book on the topic, but learned by reading other writers and drawing on what I'd picked up in other spheres. I made lots of mistakes—the way we learn. I had the vital advantage of a writer father who could answer my questions and critique my work, and whose books helped show me the way. But I gained just as much from all the non-writing I did.

Picking through trash cans? I never stopped, but simply moved from alleys to used bookstores and newspapers. Serendipity is one of the four food groups for writers. Since you never know what you'll find, it pays to keep your eyes open. That's how, in an Albuquerque used bookstore, I found the fifty-cent pamphlet on the Battle of Shiloh that led to *Bull Run*. The article about gardening as therapy that launched me on *Seedfolks* appeared in a dinky neighborhood newspaper I happened to open while eating in a bagel shop.

Building with sticks? I made a thousand found sculptures before writing my first book. I'm still making them. They were my apprenticeship in gathering, envisioning, constructing, altering, judging, revising. I still go through all these stages on every book.

Universal themes did indeed serve me well. As did turning my own material into fiction rather than memoir—until now. An event like my mother's passing became the death of Kim's father in *Seedfolks*, the abandonment at the center of *Breakout*, and much else.

Mark Twain said that the difference between the right word and the almost right word is the difference between lightning and the lightning bug. Printing showed me the importance of taking pains with details—like those little slivers of copper and brass between letters. It taught me the patience and persistence that writing requires. And when I needed a day job to pay the bills during my early writing years, it gave me that, too: I worked as a proofreader of college textbooks, making use of my trained eye for spelling and spacing.

The bicycle bequeathed me much that was crucial for writing. Authors are besieged by doubt and need a hefty supply of belief in themselves to see a book through. The cross-country trip gave me a store of self-confidence that fueled everything that followed, including the challenges of a literary career. If I made it to New Hampshire, surely I could make it through Chapter Seven. I've rarely abandoned a book. The bike also showed me I could handle solitude, another required trait, and gave me a taste of the freelance writer's life: self-contained, independent, risky, and satisfying.

The desire to see new places led me not only to sojourns in Vermont, Maine, Louisiana, North Carolina, Nebraska, France, and Mexico, but to explorations of other times and lives that inform my books. I've taken long research trips to yellow-fever-ravaged Philadelphia and Civil War Ohio, crossed the country with the naturalist John Townsend, studied silhouette cutters and pirate radio broadcasters.

History, myths, and folklore ended up informing much of my work, from *Saturnalia* and other books set in the colonial period to *Glass Slipper, Gold Sandal*, and the pairing of the *Iliad* with today's headlines in *Dateline: Troy*. Bronze spears or bullets, human nature holds true, the reason history and literature never go out of date.

The dream of composing music never died, but was channeled into books. With their orchestras of speakers, *Bull Run* and *Seedfolks* and *Seek* gave me the feeling of writing scores. It was music that led me to tell stories from multiple points of views. Hopping from recorders to alto sax, violin, mandolin, banjo, and accordion, the joy of playing with others spurred me to find ways to connect readers with each other, resulting in poems, plays, and spoken novels that were designed for performance.

You really should have been at this party.

I was lucky in the extreme. I grew up in a fun house, not the sort with tilted floors, but with magic props and musical instruments, grafting experiments in progress on the apple trees and clay in a crock if you felt like making something. My parents had no secret plan for raising creative kids but seemed just to be doing the things they loved. We were free to follow or go our own way.

In the years since, most shortwave stations have gone silent or migrated online, but there's been a revival in letterpress printing. In many cities you can take classes on how to set type and print, with no need to have all the equipment at home.

Bike touring is now mainstream, with its own magazines and a lengthening list of bike trails. For mountain bikers, there's now bikepacking.

The computer has made following along with a musical score easier than ever. Search online for a video of the piece you're after and look for results showing the image of a score. Some will even scroll along with the music. *Under Milk Wood* and *Geographical Fugue* are both easily heard online.

My father's path to page one—delightfully described in *The Abracadabra Kid: A Writer's Life*—had a plot and cast far different from mine. Yours will differ from both of ours. You might learn brainstorming through making videos or composing on GarageBand. Your adventures might be pursued in the digital realm or through ultralight backpacking or working your way around the world on organic farms.

No matter the where or the how, may the journey be rich in challenge, fairy-dusted with serendipity, and spangled with discoveries. Bon voyage!

Books

NOVELS

The Half-a-Moon Inn

Phoebe Danger, Detective: The Case of the Two-Minute Cough

Path of the Pale Horse

Rear-View Mirrors

Saturnalia

The Borning Room

Bull Run

A Fate Totally Worse Than Death

Seedfolks

Whirligig

Seek

Breakout

PICTURE BOOKS

The Birthday Tree

The Animal Hedge

Finzel the Farsighted

Rondo in C

Shadow Play

BOOKS

Time Train

Weslandia

Lost! A Story in String

Sidewalk Circus

Glass Slipper, Gold Sandal: A Worldwide Cinderella

The Dunderheads

The Dunderheads Behind Bars

The Matchbox Diary

First Light, First Life: A Worldwide Creation Story

Fearsome Giant, Fearless Child:

   A Worldwide Jack and the Beanstalk Story

POETRY

I Am Phoenix: Poems for Two Voices

Joyful Noise: Poems for Two Voices

Big Talk: Poems for Four Voices

PLAYS

Mind's Eye

Zap

SHORT STORIES

Graven Images: Three Stories

Coming-and-Going Men: Four Tales

NONFICTION

Townsend's Warbler

Copier Creations

Cannibal in the Mirror

Dateline: Troy

Eyes Wide Open: Going Behind the Environmental Headlines

Awards

The Half-a-Moon Inn 1981 Golden Kite Honor Book (SCBWI)

Graven Images 1983 Newbery Honor Book (ALA)

Joyful Noise 1988 Boston Globe–Horn Book Honor Book

    1989 Newbery Medal (ALA)

Saturnalia 1990 Boston Globe–Horn Book Honor Book

Bull Run 1994 Scott O'Dell Award for Historical Fiction

Seedfolks 1998 Golden Kite Honor Book (SCBWI)

    1998 Jane Addams Children's Book Award, Honor Book

Whirligig 1999 Golden Kite Honor Book (SCBWI)

Weslandia 2000 PEN Center USA Literary Award

    2002 California Young Reader Medal

Breakout 2003 National Book Award Finalist

The Dunderheads 2010 PEN Center USA Literary Award

The Matchbox Diary 2014 Christopher Award

Eyes Wide Open 2014 Los Angeles Times Book Prize Finalist

    2015 Green Earth Book Award (The Nature Generation)

    2014 Sigurd F. Olson Nature Writing Award

✦ ✦ ✦

For the author's body of work: 2012 Hans Christian Andersen
Award, U.S. author nominee (USBBY)

Index